Irene Forsythe Hanson

Mrs. Perry (Irene) Hanson
Westminster Gardens
1420 Santa Domingo Drive
Duarte, California 91010

The Wheelbarrow and the Comrade

Dedicated to you
Searching for real meaning in life,

Discovering a new dimension by loving
and being loved by another race,

Sharing the laughter, joy, contentment,
surprise, and high adventure of Christ
living through you—

Wherever you go!

The Wheelbarrow and the Comrade

by
IRENE HANSON

with

BERNARD PALMER

MOODY PRESS

CHICAGO

© 1973 by
THE MOODY BIBLE INSTITUTE
OF CHICAGO

ISBN: 0-8024-9428-5

About the Artwork

The silhouette cutouts were made at the Women's Bible School in Chefoo, China, and are in the folk art tradition of ancient China. To make these silhouettes, several sheets of paper are held tightly together with a pattern laid on top. The pattern is followed by jabbing down with tiny curved knives. The cutouts are then incorporated into Christmas cards and note paper.

My appreciation to Mrs. Florence L. Logan for supplying the cutouts used as illustrations in this book.

Preface

This book is a "wheelbarrow ride" through old China and will take you through humorous, surprising, and even frightening adventures. God plays the leading role in this story, as He breaks through barriers of custom, prejudices, and self-will into the lives of the Chinese. Unexpected happenings surprised me with new insights into my Christian belief.

The events take place in Shantung province, an area largely un-Westernized and untouched by the gospel. This account comes from twenty-five years of living months at a time in the interior villages where I saw only Chinese. My co-workers spoke no English. I had to speak Chinese in order to survive. Adopted into a Chinese family as "daughter" to a radiant Christian woman, I became closely linked with the Chinese people.

The Sino-Japanese War touched my life; and my final two years in China were under the communist regime, when I was accused of being an American spy and actually saw plots formed to kill me.

The Wheelbarrow and the Comrade bears my deep love and respect for a great people, as well as concern for the events of recent times.

1

I sat in the massive teak chair, a hand carved remnant of an earlier, more peaceful day and looked into the tortured eyes of the intense young Chinese man across from me. Surprisingly, I felt little emotion other than pity.

For weeks the loudspeakers along the streets of our city had been frantic in their cry of hate against me, the only symbol still remaining of the hated America. Their accusations would have been laughable were they not so serious.

"Death to the imperialist spy!" the speakers blared. "That foreign teacher is polluting our soil. She is the great American spy and must be killed!"

Of all persons, I was the last to have the qualifications for espionage; but in those days reason was gone, wiped out by the angry railing of the mob, and no one could predict what might happen.

Even now the radio was continuing its propaganda, whipping the people to frenzied hatred, and screaming for violence against the so-called enemies of the people. The sounds of a great, unruly crowd in the street, for a moment blotting out the drone of radio speakers from every corner, meant that still another government parade was being formed.

Such noisy demonstrations were supposed to be spontaneous, the volcanic eruption of enthusiasm for the new regime. Actually, they were well planned and executed. Even the timing bore the stamp of similarity that marked so many of their propaganda efforts.

My attention, diverted briefly by the tumult outside, was forced back to my bewildered guest. To hear his anguished admission was not surprising, nor was I greatly disturbed by it. God gave me an overwhelming love that wiped out any resentment or anger I might have held for Lee Ahn, our mission's Chinese business manager. It was as though His hand was upon me, easing my concern. Looking back, I do not think there has ever been a time when I have had such complete trust and joy in my Saviour.

I was aware of my own precarious situation from the time the Communists first took over our city. I knew there might be some sort of personal danger when I elected to remain behind after the other missionaries were evacuated.

"I'm not married," I remembered telling those who counseled me to leave. "It's better for me to stay behind than for a man with a wife and small children to do so. And, someone should be here to help with the Chinese church."

At first I was not bothered, except for the official calls and meetings to explain the new regulations. The government was concentrating on gaining control of the country and solidifying their position.

But, after some months I discovered that I had not been forgotten by the Communists. The regulations tightened and the government-controlled radio unleashed a cry against me. I was an American spy, they shouted, and an enemy of the people. I had to be destroyed. As the tempo of their accusations increased, I knew it would not be long until there was a move against me.

I knew Lee Ahn had been arrested a few weeks before and had been put through intensive Communist thought-conditioning, but we had talked about it at length after his release. I marveled at the way he had resisted their indoctrination. Now I saw that they had been able to accomplish more than I had realized.

Slowly he raised his head, the hurt deep in his eyes.

"I had to come and tell you before it happens," he repeated as though the horror of what he was about to do could be lessened by the telling. "It is your life or mine. I have to be *your* Judas!"

At first I did not understand.

"The last thing they said to me before they let me go was that I have to obey their orders in the future or they will kill me."

"I see."

"And just today I got my instructions. I have to make a public accusation against you! It means your life!"

So that was it. Although the Communists were ruthless in their dealings with those they felt to be enemies of the state, they went to great lengths to present a facade of legality to their executions in an effort to make the world believe they were establishing a just and responsible government. They wanted to kill me but had to make it appear to be the result of an ordered legal process. And this was the method they had chosen. One of our own was being used against me.

"I have no one who depends on me, Lee Ahn," I said as gently as possible. "You have your family and the church. They both need you."

"But don't you *see?*" he cried in agony. "I *have* to do it!"

"I know that."

He waited, as though for me to continue, but I could say nothing for a time; and when I was able to speak, my words were of little comfort.

"You are the one who must decide what you will do."

His groan of despair chilled me. His lips trembled and his entire being shook. I wanted to help him, but what could

9

I say to lessen the pain he was experiencing? His gaze came up to meet mine. Then a horrible, agonizing scream escaped his lips, unlike any sound I had ever heard or imagined; and he jumped to his feet. He stared at me, his face twisted, and burst from the house, leaving the door ajar.

For a moment I was stunned motionless by what had happened. Only the ticking of the clock on the wall pierced my consciousness. Finally I stirred myself and, scarcely aware of my action, I went out and shut the door behind me, the uncertainty and turmoil of recent weeks exploding within.

From where I stood, I could look out over the courtyard wall to the street below where the parade was approaching. It was another of those cleverly contrived orgies of violence designed to replace reason with fear and judgment with blind obedience.

I didn't have to look. I had seen it all before, more times than I remembered. There was the mob surging up the street with their banners and slogans and their effigies of Uncle Sam and Chiang Kai-shek. There were the cymbals and drums and the shoutings of hate. Yet, there was a fascination in all of this that held me at the window even as the noise grew louder and more uncontrolled. I was disturbed yet strangely peaceful.

What was this monster that was wrapping its tentacles of death and ruin about my beloved China? What was it that had caught up Lee Ahn and myself and was about to crush us? What was going to happen to that sensitive young Christian who was experiencing such agony because he was being forced to turn against me?

"Oh, God," I prayed, "I have served You out here for twenty-five years. Is this to be the end? Am I no longer to see Your love break through people and circumstances to work Your will? What do You have for me now? Are You going to take me home to You or do You have a prison cell waiting?"

I wanted His will, whatever it was, but it was difficult to think about leaving my work and these people I loved so much.

Twenty-five years?

In a way it seemed forever. Home in America was wonderful, yes, but I had only faint memories of it. My real life had actually begun in China.

The Communists, the parade, and even the threat of death on the testimony of the tortured Lee Ahn faded from my mind. My ears closed out the tumult that was boiling along the street below and I was back in Shanghai, one of a group of newly arriving Presbyterian missionaries in 1926.

Our ship was churning into the wide, rolling Yangtze River that sprawls into the heart of Asia like the traditional Chinese dragon—a great, turbulent artery, yellow with the soil of ages. The Yangtze stretches across China to the outer reaches of Mongolia, leaching away the life-producing soil and belching the thickening mass of mud and water through a mouth sixty-five miles wide into the Yellow Sea.

I stood on the deck alone, leaning on the railing and looking to the distant pencil line of flat land and low dwellings. Slowly the pencil line thickened. Villages became visible and the ever present junks, those distinctive Chinese sailing vessels, dotted the water around us.

I knew only one Chinese phrase, taught to me by one of the other single girls in our party.

"Deng-i-deng," I rolled it off my tongue self-consciously. "Deng-i-deng. Wait a minute."

The phrase didn't sound like words at all. Would I ever be able to learn such a strange, singsong language? Would I be able to make the adjustment to a people whose ways were so different than ours?

We were slowing down beside a long wharf. My senses were assailed by an uproar of strange sounds, overpowering odors, and the constant motion of innumerable carts and people—a turbulent sea of yellow-skinned, black-haired, dark-eyed people.

Very soon after docking, the mission treasurer, an American, came aboard to bring us Chinese money for our immediate needs. Then the representative of the missionary home where we would be staying came to us. A tall, spotless Chinese with a calm, radiant face, he said, "Give me the keys to your trunks and bags! I will take them through customs. Come to the office at three o'clock this afternoon, and I will return your keys."

What! Give up my keys to this stranger! What would happen to my possessions? But that marvellous face! I yielded my keys.

That afternoon at three o'clock I went to the office of the missionary home. The man with the almost sublime face asked me no questions. He handed me my keys and pointed to my luggage. All was in perfect order.

I shall never forget his face and the contrast it was to other faces around me in that new land. No fear, no turmoil in that face. Could it be that he was a Chinese Christian? I learned later that he was.

Several days later, while we were going from the ship dock in Tientsin to Peking and language school, I had my first evidence of God's tender mercy and guidance since our arrival in China. I was the first to get into a ricksha. The instant I did so, the young ricksha man sped away without even waiting to be told where I wanted to go.

Panicking, I looked behind. The others were nowhere in sight. I was in a strange city alone. I knew but a single phrase of Chinese among a people who did not speak English. A thousand fearful thoughts crowded in. Where was I being taken? What would the ricksha man do with me?

And then I remembered. *"Deng-i-deng!"* I called out, using the only Chinese phrase I knew. "Wait a minute!"

He stopped instantly, intent only on serving me. Soon

the others caught up, and we continued on together to the railroad station.

I thought about that incident often in the days that followed. It was only a minor happening, a brief interlude that caused me a bit of anxiety, but God in His compassion for a frightened girl had provided me with the one Chinese phrase I needed. I began to see that He held me in His hand and nothing could happen that He did not permit.

2

The excellent language school filled our schedule with interesting teachers who made learning the complex language an adventure. But it was still a task.

The teachers were not allowed to speak any English to us. We began as children do, by hearing the sound and guessing at the meaning. A charming head teacher made the presentation with pictures and clever acting. Small groups and private sessions provided practice. Later we had lesson sheets with the Chinese written character, the English spelling for the sound, and the English meaning.

The writing was not alphabetical but a high form of art. Fantastic pictures of ideas, centuries old, often carried a moral thought. For instance, *dependable* or *trustworthy* was represented by a character combining two other characters: a man standing, and words coming out of the mouth. Thus, the character literally meant that a man could stand on (or believe) the spoken word. Many words were less clear and more complicated, yet writing was fun.

All sounds had four tones, each with a different meaning.

The same sound could mean a dress, soap, choir, or righteousness; the tone—flat, high level, rising, or falling—made the difference. Several meanings had the same tone; for instance, to heal, to film, to groan, and to bow. Then the meaning could only be known by the context of the sentence.

During those early months in China we must have been a difficulty to the merchants and ricksha men in the area and to anyone else who had to deal with us. One of my classmates was riding in a ricksha when she saw something in a shop she wanted.

"*Ching tsoa,*" she called out, drawing from her first lesson which was the only Chinese she knew. "*Ching tsoa.* Please sit down."

On another occasion a friend and I went to buy some Eagle Brand condensed milk. For some reason that was the only kind of milk that would do.

"We want—," my friend began. And then, because she did not know the words for milk, she pointed to the tins on the shelf.

The merchant could understand our gesture, so we got milk, but not the right brand.

"Not this kind," I answered, expending another phrase. Then I stopped, not knowing what to say or do next.

"We want this kind," my friend said, flapping her arms like a bird.

"*Yu, yu!* I have it! I have it!" The laughing storekeeper ran to the back of the shop and brought out the Eagle Brand milk.

Those were exciting months for all of us. Now I wonder how we got through them. Even more, I have wondered how our instructors were able to hammer even a few of the fundamentals of the language into us.

Thinking we could learn Chinese more quickly and also get a better grasp of the culture of those ancient and dignified people, my friend and I left the school hostel to live in

15

the beautiful home of a highly educated scholar and official under the former emperor.

In a home such as that, it was important that we learn to eat properly so we would not offend our hosts or embarrass them by our poor manners. We soon mastered the use of chopsticks and the correct way to hold our rice bowl with one thumb on the top.

We found the ways of the educated Chinese, such as those who frequented the home of our host, intriguing. Neither my friend nor I had ever seen such dignity or courtesy, such consideration for the welfare and enjoyment of guests.

One night our host and his wife were taking us in rickshas to see a display of fireworks for the Chinese New Year when our host met a friend of equal status. The rickshas stopped, and the men, both wearing the same kind of flowing silk robes, got down and faced each other. Then, taking off their glasses, they bowed slowly and with deep respect.

The glasses, I learned, are considered a barrier, and the two men were friends and wanted nothing to be between them. Knowing that, I was later able to understand why one pastor reverently removed his glasses whenever he led in prayer. He did not want anything between himself and God.

Life in their home was quiet and pleasant, and we found ourselves enjoying it; but the forces of change were at work— change that had its roots in the past. Since 1911 when the Manchu dynasty was overthrown, China had been seething with unrest.

Dr. Sun Yat-sen planned for self-rule, but the Republic came into being before either he or the people were ready for it, a flower that bloomed while snow still lay on the ground and the bite of frost was in the air. It was doomed, even before it began to function.

The fledgling government soon began to lose its tenuous hold on the nation, and unity disintegrated like a sand castle on the beach when the tide rolls in. It wasn't long until the country broke apart with warlords controling the provinces and battling savagely with one another.

Chaos was near.

Sun Yat-sen, the father of the Manchu overthrow, battled valiantly to achieve national unity; but to do that he had to subdue the factious warlords. He brought in Russian advisers to train the new army under the leadership of the brilliant young commander, Chiang Kai-shek. He got the military assistance he sought and more. Along with the advisers came the political and propaganda cadres, which set to work cautiously.

The Communist party came into being .

A feeble child in those early years, it could have died of neglect and malnutrition. So weak was its hold on life that it scarcely attracted the attention of anyone. But in the vacuum that was China in those days, it managed to survive, spreading its false promise of equality and a better day among the disadvantaged and the young. Even the idealistic Chiang Kai-shek subscribed at first to its principles.

His new army took Canton and began its northern march, reaching Nanking in early 1927. There the hate slogans of the Communists exploded into violence. The cry went up, "Kill Americans!"

Homes were looted, property was destroyed, and at least one missionary was killed. A massacre was narrowly averted when others miraculously escaped to American ships in the harbor.

Chang Kai-shek broke with the Communists. They tried unsuccessfully to overthrow him, and open civil war followed.

The antiforeigner feeling spread so rapidly and became so critical that the American government ordered all missionaries to leave the interior. The Chinese were equally anxious to see us go because they did not want the United States involved in their civil war.

17

Some missionaries went to Japan and some, convinced that any return to China was impossible in the foreseeable future, returned to America. My trust in God was that He had called me to China and that I would be permitted to go back there someday. The mission sent me to Korea, along with a number of others.

We were taken north of the Great Wall of China by train, going through Manchuria. In the railway station where we changed trains, I saw crowds of people dressed in white cotton clothes. The Chinese I was used to seeing wore blue or black.

I made a mistake common to strangers who were new to the Orient, carrying over customs of one culture to another.

"My, what a big funeral!" I remarked to my companions, because the Chinese reserved white as the color for mourning and funerals. Later I learned that the Koreans always wore white.

We went to central Korea where we were taken into the homes of other missionaries. It didn't seem to disturb Dr. and Mrs. Reynolds that we were from a different denomination or that they would have four of us to care for. They even planned to move their family into the basement and the attic to give us the more comfortable rooms of their homes. (Of course we could not have permitted that.) Fortunately, it did not prove to be necessary.

In that home I saw much openheartedness. They were an example of the fellowship believers have in Christ and should show to each other.

Studying was still my principal task and I continued long hours each day with a Chinese teacher, preparing for my coming examination. There was work for me to do in that country, and the Korean Mission invited me to transfer my credentials there and begin language studies, but I had given my heart to China. In all the time I was there, I only learned one brief sentence in their language: "I do not speak Korean."

Korea was a small country with the land area of only one of China's provinces and less population. All Korea showed the results of intense missionary work, fully organized and adequately staffed. At a time of national humiliation and severe oppression, the Koreans had turned with sincere commitment to all that Christ offers. In their churches they found freedom of spirit, places of leadership, and real meaning in life—all of which were denied them in their national life. God had a unique opportunity to break through.

The church in that poor nation was a joy and a source of amazement. I could not understand a word in the services, yet I felt a oneness of fellowship in being with them.

The meetings began very early in the morning and ran on continuously. The people were poor, but their Sunday clothes were spotless as they came in and sat on the floor, which was so clean it shone. Their faces were radiant and shining, like the face of the Chinese man in Shanghai. The women were on one side of the sanctuary, and the men on the other. The headdresses of the northern women were tied in such a way that the ends, four or five inches long, stood out on either side at the backs of their heads. They reminded me of a great flock of white doves, wings spread and glinting in the sunlight, as they were about to come to rest on the ground.

The reverence of the people and their singing stirred me in an unusual way. It was there that I realized love can be felt, especially the love of God, and that the Holy Spirit knows no language barriers. I looked forward to those services and felt I was a part of them even though I was not able to understand one word.

I was still in Korea when the cable came telling of my father's death. And I hadn't even known that he had been ill.

The concern of the other missionaries was comforting in the weeks that followed, but not immediately. I wanted to be alone, away from the eyes of others. I wanted to be able to cry without making the others sad—to pour out my heart to God. As soon as I could, I left them and made my way to the top of the nearby mountain.

Away from the noise and confusion of the city I found strength in my Lord. On the crest of that great hill the deep quiet comforted me.

At first I did not even pray.

Strangely, I thought of the Chinese temples which were always built on high elevations, as though to satisfy an inner longing of man to get above the cares of the world, even in idol worship. It was the same of the heathen religions mentioned so often in the Old Testament. Their altars and sacred groves were usually on the high places.

As I stood there alone I thought I could understand why man always had climbed to the highest spots in order to worship. Only, I had more than the serenity of the mountain to give me peace and courage. I had the arms of the living God.

Where could the people of China turn for help in the loss of a loved one? To their god shelves? Buddha? The wisdom of Confucius? But for the Lord Jesus Christ, I would be as empty and hopeless as they in this time of heartache and sorrow.

Sitting down on a grassy spot some distance from the path, I began to think of home. My brothers and sisters would be with Mother in Oregon, along with our many other relatives. I would be the only one missing. Father and I.

The two of us had always been close. Closer, perhaps, than we were with other members of the family. There was that peculiar oneness of spirit that seems to bind certain people together. His heart was in the soil; and I had found particular enjoyment in being out with him, helping him tend his three and one-half acres of loganberries. I had helped him pick them in the spring and delivered them for him with the car while he did other things.

He had a marvelous sense of humor, which I appreciated more than I realized until this moment. We were constantly joking as we worked, and when he heard a good story he wrote it in his memory with a firm, sure hand so he would be sure to remember it to share with me. Occasionally I had overslept. When that happened and I didn't come down for breakfast, he would waken me with a joke shouted from the kitchen. Just being with him had been so much fun.

Now all of that was over. The news seemed to have an unreal quality about it, as though it hadn't actually happened. But that cold impersonal cable was true. There was no mistaking it. I faced it up on that mountain.

I could never forget the look on Father's face when I told him of my decision to go to China as a missionary.

There was such joy and pride in his face it made my heart ache. Thinking back, I could still hear him making excuses to tell new acquaintances and strangers where his daughter was going, and why. And if any doubted the wisdom of my decision he was the first to defend me.

If he had been thinking only of himself I'm sure he would have preferred that I stay at home where we could enjoy each other's company. But, as much as he loved his family and wanted them to be with him, he loved the Lord Jesus Christ even more.

Now Father was gone.

Self-pity washed over me in great, surging waves and I was the most desolate person in the world. In that moment it would have been easy for me to have decided God had forsaken me. Then Psalm 91 which Father read to me when I was ready to leave home came back to comfort me: *"He will keep you in perfect peace."*

Father's faith had been the cornerstone of his life—the constant guide for every situation, every trouble, every heartache. Desperately I clung to that verse, wringing all the help that I, in my weakness and grief, could find in it.

21

Yet, I could not help asking myself why it had happened. Why did God permit my father to die?

Then another verse came to me to help ease my aching spirit: "The God of all comfort . . . comforteth us in all our tribulation, that we may be able to comfort them which are in any trouble, by the comfort wherewith we ourselves are comforted of God" (2 Co 1:3, 4).

Perhaps God did have a purpose in taking my father home to be with Him. I still could not understand the reason. I could only accept what God's highest love brought.

"Dear God," I prayed, my soul crying out to Him in an anguish that could not be expressed in words. "I know this in Your will. I'm too weak to understand, but help me to accept what has happened and to thank and praise You for it."

It was not easy! Those same tormenting questions pounded again and again at the very depths of my being, but that hour on the mountain gave me a victory over grief that I never would before have believed possible. Christ's presence and comfort were very near in that moment of need and in the months that followed. When my personal loss threatened to overwhelm me, I could go back in memory to my meeting with Christ on the Korean mountaintop and gain the strength I needed to carry on.

3

The news from China was encouraging. The unrest was subsiding as the Nationalist Army extended its control from one province to another, bringing the warlords under subjection and scattering the fledgling Communists. As that happened, the anti-Americanism that had reared its ugly head only a short time before began to subside. In late spring the mission authorities decided it was safe for us to return.

At first only the men were permitted to go into the interior, but this was to be changed as soon as practicable. The men were desperately needed at their stations. The Chinese Christian leaders were devout enough but had not been wholly prepared for the responsibility of caring for the church in this crisis that was so suddenly thrust upon them. In many areas the work was faltering badly.

For some of the women, and especially for those with husbands and small children, the separation would be difficult, despite the fact that they recognized the need for caution.

They would carry on as best they could in coastal areas until experience showed that it would be safe for them to rejoin their husbands.

As far as I personally was concerned, however, it made but little difference. It was still language school for me.

A temporary language school had been set up in the coastal city where I was now staying, so I was able to continue my classes. And I lived in a large house with three other first-term missionaries. It was enjoyable but Chinese was not coming as rapidly as I thought it should, and for good reason.

I lived with Americans and spoke English, except at school or while doing my homework. There was little opportunity for me to practice my faulty Chinese, to sharpen my pronunciation on the friendly criticism of the Chinese themselves. I lacked the constant pressure of necessity.

So I found an ordinary home to take me in as a boarder. I was happier there and my progress in the complex tonal language increased almost immediately. And when that happened, my spirits picked up. Perhaps I would be able to learn Chinese after all.

In the fall of my second year the time finally came that I was to be given a permanent assignment. Temporary language school had ended. Missionaries were all returning to the interior. Families were reunited. Great excitement took hold of me as I went to the missionary meeting. I soon would be at work bringing Christ to these people I had grown to love. It didn't seem possible.

My assignment sounded routine enough, as a missionary with a map briefed me. The province where I would be stationed was large and densely populated, with 640 people living on each square mile. Its huge, walled cities boasted histories stretching back into antiquity. There were innumerable market towns, governmental centers, and endless villages—all seething with people. The map on the platform had the area where I would be working designated as "well evangelized."

I stared at the speaker. The facts he presented were startling. There were 3,000 believers, but there were hundreds of villages and towns with only one or two Christians. And more than 4,000 were completely untouched, which meant that there was no general knowledge among the people of even the name of Jesus Christ. In many of those villages no one had ever seen a foreigner.

"And you call this area 'well evangelized'?" I could not contain myself.

"I'm only speaking by comparison," he told me. "We have twenty-seven organized churches and about the same number of preaching places and unorganized groups. Other missions are also working in the area."

I was still unconvinced.

"Compared to Tibet and Mongolia, our area is well evangelized," he replied.

The coastal city that served as headquarters for our missionary effort in that area had a language school that would permit me to continue my ever continuing studies. There were two high schools where work could be done and there were also the usual activities of a city, but they were not thinking of using me in either place. They wanted me to help plow new ground, to do pioneer work in the towns and villages.

I would not be working alone, I was told. Two Chinese women evangelists, seminary-trained, would be assisting me. They were charming young women from long-established Christian families. In addition to their help with the work, they would be assisting me as I was striving to learn the ways and customs of my strange new world. It had been years since a woman had lived for much time out in the area and never with such trained Chinese co-workers. Later, other stations wished they had our setup.

25

Not having the responsibilities of a home and family gave us certain advantages in the sort of work we would be doing. No doubt that had been a factor in our being chosen for village work. We would be free to live out for extended intervals, going where we were needed and staying as long as it seemed wise and profitable.

Our work, I was told, would be most varied. In one village the church would be well established and the Christians there stable, respected members of the community. In another there would be but a single believer, persecuted and lonely for fellowship and acceptance by the clan.

"And, of course," he went on, "we are also hopeful that you will be able to get into this untouched area and begin to make friends and witness to these people." He outlined it on the map.

I was all but submerged by the conflicting emotions that rolled over me. Anticipation and excitement trembled within. At last I would be able to begin what I had come to China for. I could scarcely wait. Yet I knew so little about approaching the Chinese about Christ.

How was I going to relate to a people whose ways were so different from my own? How could I help them with problems I so dimly understood myself? I was so weak and insecure, and so lacking in wisdom. How could I make them see Christ living in me?

And what would those two cultured, well-educated young Chinese women I would be working with think of me? They were so respected by their own people for their education that they were always addressed formally as Miss Heng and Miss Leu. I was educated, too, but I was still the same girl who picked loganberries with her father and was awakened by his jokes when I slept in. Would I be dignified enough for them?

At that moment I would not have gone back to America if I could. A whole new world was ahead.

Still I was glad for the help of the two Chinese women. So much would be expected of me as a missionary, and I knew so little. I hoped I would be wise enough to learn from them.

"Oh, yes," the mission representative went on, eyes dancing. "There's one more thing. Have you ever ridden a wheelbarrow?"

A wheelbarrow? It had been years since I had even seen one, that I could recall. He had to be joking.

But he didn't seem to be. The smile slipped away from his face, leaving him serious. "There are some graveled and paved roads in our province for buses and carts," he continued, "but thousands of villages can be reached only by narrow paths. And you'll get so weary you'll have to ride a wheelbarrow. You'd better learn to like it."

"Nothing drab about being a missionary," I smiled.

The two young women who were to accompany me came to see me before the week was out. They, too, were entering a new life and were approaching it with a sense of excitement and apprehension, not knowing what to expect from me or from the next few months we would be spending together.

They were both shorter than I. Miss Leu was slight and stylishly dressed, while Miss Heng was built on a broader scale, maintaining the traditional Chinese garments.

Miss Leu was the gay one. Her eyes danced with the excitement of each new hour. She was quick to laugh, slow to frown, and sang beautifully. Miss Heng's black eyes looked seriously at me from a round, olive face that was calm and appealing. I soon discovered that she was the more studious of the two, given to carrying a Bible with her, or a book or magazine so she could read if she had to wait a few minutes. She was sensitive to people and their needs, and knew how to make Christ relevant to them. Miss Leu chattered constantly, good humor and the joy of living bubbling within until she could not remain silent.

The girls had been classmates in high school and seminary. They both came from solid Christian homes and shared the same love for Jesus Christ and compassion for those without Him.

We made a strange trio. They were so different from each other, and I was different than either of them. I could wear the dark blue cotton trousers and dress they instructed the tailor to make for me, but I couldn't change my pale skin and hair and round blue eyes.

My companions helped me get the things I needed for the trip. I had to have a *lantzu,* a big metal-strengthened basket about three feet long and half that wide, cooking utensils, and food. Some things would be available in the villages on market days. Others would have to be taken along. I also needed a flat canvas bedroll and a lantern. And of course, with three more years of language examinations ahead, a Chinese teacher had to go with us, too.

When I put on my new Chinese clothes, Miss Heng and Miss Leu surveyed me critically. They were most particular about my dress, knowing the importance of being clothed conventionally and in a proper manner for the area and position of the people with whom we would be working. And, they wanted to be proud of me. I was glad they cared that much.

My associates tried to prepare me for what we would find. There was no electricity or refrigeration, and no modern laborsaving devices. The markets, held once every five days, were miles apart, and the buying was a ritual of haggling over prices, a game both the buyer and seller played with varying degrees of skill. Running water was unheard of, and so were individual wells. Large drums of the precious liquid were carried on shoulder poles from the village well. Even in our headquarters city, messages went by hand for lack of a telephone. A servant to look after our needs under such conditions was indispensable and showed us unmatched loyalty and devotion.

Before we left on our trip, the director of the station came with a letter from one church that had written asking our assistance. There were other churches nearby that would be needing our help as well. He had included a list of them.

"You haven't ridden on a wheelbarrow, have you?" His laughter followed our ricksha as we left to go to the railway station.

"Are the wheelbarrows *that* bad?" I asked Miss Leu uneasily.

"You'll see." Those lights pirouetted in her eyes again. "You'll see."

The trains were crowded, and everywhere that we looked out the window there were walled towns and villages surrounded by well-marked field plots. The towns were jammed, almost one against the other, a village to the mile, or so it seemed. And the thatched-roof houses were built wall to wall, crowded together like the junks in the Shanghai harbor. The Chinese farmers lived in the walled villages for protection against bandits and thieves and went out to the land during the day to farm. A few of the more fortunate had a mule or a donkey to help with the work. The others pulled their plows or wheelbarrows themselves.

I shuddered. "Do they have to do that?" I asked. My body ached for them.

"Oh, yes." Miss Heng saw it as a fact of life. She knew the burden but also knew their wiry tenacious strength. I had seen men pulling plows or rickshas, too, but it still tugged at my heart. I couldn't help wondering how I would feel if my father had had to work so hard.

We transferred from the train to the bus and finally to a wheelbarrow to cover the remaining distance. Our helper bargained for the wheelbarrow, shaking his head and gesturing as though the stranger whose services he was seeking had suddenly become an enemy. Then an understanding was reached. Voices lowered and smiles came. I was ready for my first wheelbarrow ride.

The wheelbarrow had one center wooden wheel about three feet high with a wooden framework over it and extending out to the side. The flat bedroll was untied and unrolled to cushion the seat on one side for the rider and the luggage was packed in such a way that it balanced the weight surprisingly well. A man with a firm, woven strap about three inches wide over his shoulder pushed the wheelbarrow and managed the mule which was pulling. Other barrow pushers had donkeys or, if they were very poor, another man to help with the cumbersome vehicle. A good barrow man, I learned, could cover three miles an hour, or thirty miles on a long summer day. Engineers have explained that the wheelbarrow has excellent balance enabling it to carry great weights. I learned that there were barrow trains of great numbers which carried immense loads for hundreds of miles.

"Double up your legs," Miss Leu instructed me, giggling, "and sit still."

"How can I do that?"

Her laughter trilled. "Try not to wiggle."

I climbed into place gingerly and hung on as the high, squeaking falsetto of the strange vehicle screeched in my ears.

"The best way to ride a wheelbarrow," I told my companions when we finally reached our destination, "is to walk."

But Miss Heng was wiser than I. "Before we get back to the city you will thank God for the wheelbarrow," she prophesied.

4

Our first evangelistic trip took us to a village where the church was well established. The Christians knew we were coming and had been waiting expectantly. The men were dressed in the same white summer shirts and loose black trousers we had seen in Peking and our headquarters' city; and the women wore the traditional blue trousers under three-quarter-length white or blue blouses buttoned on the sides.

They came forward to greet us, smiling their welcome, and escorted us to a cleanly swept courtyard surrounded by a high stone wall. Inside was a stone-walled house with a thatched roof. I wondered if the place was empty and was to be our home while we were with them, but I did not ask. I had learned to allow my companions to take the initiative so I would not blunder against the customs of the people.

31

Miss Leu pressed close to me as we entered the large center room with its little window along the north wall. "My, this is luxury," she whispered.

I looked around without comment. The house would be comfortable enough, it was true. But I could not have called it luxurious, even for the Orient where houses were so different from ours.

At each end of the large room there was a door leading to a bedroom; at the south side of each bedroom door there was a low stove. On the other side of the stove was a large window for light, facing the courtyard. I found the stoves fascinating. They consisted of a large iron kettle set in a brick framework, built against the bedroom wall. The flue went into the bedroom.

"How does that work?" I asked when I was alone with my companions.

Miss Leu answered, "Come here and I'll show you."

There was a brick platform about three feet high, five feet wide, and as long as the room along the south side of the bedroom, covered with a clean, shiny mat. A large window, level with the platform, looked out on the courtyard to the south.

"Is that platform what I think it is?" I asked.

"It's a *kang*, a bed."

I soon discovered that the flue of the kitchen stove passed under the platform, the smoke heating the bed before going on to the outside chimney. There was no other means of heating the room. It didn't look adequate to me, but I decided it must be. Such beds, I knew, were used all over north China.

Miss Leu showed me how to use the stove, sitting cross-legged on the mat in front of it and holding dry cornstalks or grass (wood was scarce in that area) up to the bottom of the kettle. The stove was used for everything: heating water, making cereal, steaming bread, and cooking meat and vegetables.

"If this house weren't empty, we'd live here with the family. They would empty out a bedroom and allow us to use the stove at the end."

Guests were coming across the courtyard to visit. Miss Leu finished hurriedly in a low whisper. "Now we have the whole house to ourselves. That's why I said it was luxury."

We ushered our women guests into the bedroom where we sat on the flat, hard Chinese bed. I couldn't cross my legs as the others did, quickly and easily tucking them under the loose top blouse. Mine stuck awkwardly out in front of me. I was very conscious of the fact that I was not sitting properly, but they were gracious and said nothing.

There was a purpose for the visit.

"If you aren't too weary from the trip," the spokesman said, "the Elder hopes you can meet with us in the church in a little while."

Too weary? That was what we had come for! We would not have missed it!

The church, we discovered, was a nicer building than the one we were living in. The brick structure with its tile roof was larger and higher than our house, and its whitewashed interior gleamed. When we got there, the backless benches were filled and the Elder, a dignified gentleman scholar, was on the platform.

"We have come to welcome our distinguished guests today," he began in the time-honored gentility of the people. "We are most happy to have these important friends with us. They are with us to teach us more of Jesus Christ and to lead us to know Him better. The teacher has come all the way from America and we know already that we will love her. As for the young seminary graduates who are with her, some of us are related to them. And their families are well-known friends to the rest of us. We are all delighted with their presence."

When the welcoming speech was over, the elders of the church appeared with teapots, cups, and cakes to serve us.

I didn't realize the significance of what was happening until I heard the guarded whispers of the women behind me.

"This is something I have never seen before. It's the first time the men in our village have ever served the women."

"It wouldn't happen if we weren't Christian."

They had seen the elders serve communion regularly, but this was a social event. To everyone, it was a new experience. I couldn't help thinking that only Christ gave women dignity and self-respect and their rightful position in life.

But the tea party was not over. We were expected to speak briefly to the group, expressing our thanks. When my turn came, I did the best I could, stumbling over the words and feeling a sense of my own inadequacy. When I finished, the Elder rose again.

"Since you are new to our country, I would like to tell you about the early beginnings of our church." He paused, glancing at the younger ones in the building. "I imagine there are many of you who haven't heard this story either."

The story began in the late 1800s, or so he thought. A non-Christian sect had sprung into being with a widely scattered following. They had a book they based their religion on. And though they weren't Christian, there was a certain morality about them and they were sincere in what they believed. For some reason the government disbanded them as criminals.

One of the members in the mountains heard that in the north of the province there was a teacher who also had a book. Curious, he sent men to walk the two hundred miles to seek out the teacher and inquire about his religion.

"Our book said that someday a great teacher would come," they told the missionary. "We have been waiting for him. Will you teach us from your book?"

The missionary was delighted, especially when he learned that they had followers in nine towns, all eager to hear.

"That missionary came and worked among us, in spite of the official and family-opposition pressures that always followed him. Some refused to sell him food or water. In one village they cut off the tail of his horse and put stones under his saddle. But nine churches grew out of those nine groups of believers."

He waited as though to give us time to think about what he had said.

"That man had a tremendous heart of love and the people loved him in return. Worthy teacher, you are following his path. Only you will go like a queen and be treated with great courtesy and respect. You will not be persecuted.

"From here you will go to the mountain village where that missionary first began to work among us. It is unique. There is not a temple in it and there are only Christians living there. I know of no other such village in all of China."

Personal friendships were begun in those days in the village and our love for the people grew.

"It must be Christ who gives us this warm fellowship so quickly," I said to Miss Heng.

Her understanding eyes came up to meet mine. "Yes," she said, "Isn't it wonderful?"

We were busy while we were at the village, holding regular Bible studies and times of singing and prayer. And, for me, there were the inevitable language lessons.

How necessary they were! I'm sure the Chinese members of my first classes learned little from my stumbling attempts to express myself and explain the Word of God.

One day I had finished preparing the lesson for the next day and was painfully working out the sentences in Chinese when Miss Leu and a group of Christian girls dashed into the room.

"Come see a dragon dance!"

35

The rhythmic sound of beating cymbals led us to the crowd surrounding the dragon. It was a gaudy, painted creature made of cloth covering a jointed cornstalk framework. The fierce head was made of colored paper pasted over a frame and with red paper lining its mouth. The dragon was at least fifty feet long. Balancing it on long sticks held high in the air, the men began to sway slowly to the rhythm of the cymbals, making the ugly, imaginary animal writhe realistically. Had the dance been held at night, lights would have been put in the mouth and on the joints of the body.

The dragon was the symbol of the past emperor of China and was called the god of water, rain, and thunder. In Chinese art the dragon is always shown chasing a pearl represented by a white ball. There were various explanations of the significance of the pearl. One says that it typifies the search of the heart of man for the answer to life's questions. Whether that is the true origin of the symbol or not is lost in antiquity.

The day before we were to leave, there was a wedding in the village. They did not follow the old custom of having such ceremonies at night. There were no individual invitations. Most of the people were related and everyone was expected to come. We arrived in time to hear the sonorous blast of the trumpets and the gay, lilting melody of the bagpipes as the marching band signaled the approach of the bridal party.

Following the band came two enclosed red wedding chairs gaily festooned with bright red silk and carried on the shoulders of men. We joined the crowd, following the procession to the door of the groom's home where the chairs were lowered.

The groom came out first, and he and his party entered the courtyard. Then the bride and her party did the same. She was dressed in an embroidered red silk skirt and long, loose blouse. Her traditional fancy headdress, long earrings, and face were covered by a red cloth.

The family, and as many others as could crowd in, filled the courtyard, directing their attention to the center house door where a table shrine had been set up with candles, incense, plates of white steamed bread, and a cup of wine. The oldest man of the groom's family poured the wine onto the ground. Incense was burned. After that all of the men of the groom's family bowed with heads to the ground in worship of their ancestors and heaven and earth.

The saddle that had been placed on the doorsill seemed out of place to me until I was told that the sounds for the words "saddle" and "peace" were identical. The saddle represented the hope that the bride's stepping over it into the new home and into this large family with the mother-in-law in charge, would bring peace and harmony.

Miss Heng explained to me the bride's position in her new home. Men were in authority in business matters and the farming which most of the people in that village did. Inside the home, however, it was a woman's world. Under the crowded conditions of China, separate living quarters for the new family were usually impossible. The home not only had to be shared with the groom's parents but often with the families of other sons as well.

In such a situation one person had to be in control, and that person was the mother-in-law! With limited finances and human frailties her situation was not easy, requiring great fairness and love. Some were able to discharge that responsibility and others were not. Some brides were able to accept the direction of an older woman they didn't know. Others found it difficult. That was the reason for the saddle— a hope of harmony.

I'm afraid it would take more than stepping over a saddle to make me accept the situation that girl was going into, I told myself, *and still be happy.*

After the usual courtyard worship service, the red cloth was removed from the bride's head. It was then that the bride and groom saw each other for the first time. She stepped over the saddle and was led to her bedroom, already furnished by her dowry.

The families, I learned, were actually strangers to each other. A middleman made all the arrangements. As years passed, we learned that this was the customary non-Christian service, varying little over our area. We saw many of them.

The next day we went up to the village that was entirely Christian, again by wheelbarrow. There we had another warm welcome and a second tea party served by the men for the women.

Miss Leu and Miss Heng and I were learning to live together and care for each other in our close quarters. In that village we had so little space the three of us were forced to sleep crosswise on the one bed platform.

Finishing there, we went still deeper into the mountains, riding by mule over trails so narrow and steep they frightened me. For a saddle, the bedroll was tied, but none too securely! At our third village I saw my first pagan funeral. It was haunting.

There were the inevitable bands and trumpets sounding their mournful tunes on the still mountain air, and the high-pitched, nasal wailing as the relatives and friends lamented their loss. The family mourners and arriving relatives wore long, cheap, cream-colored cotton mourning clothes, the symbols of grief.

Over on a threshing floor, by which the procession paused, tables were set and filled with bowls of cooked foods—fish, chickens, a whole pig's head, and small loaves of steamed bread. This food would be washed and recooked after the ceremony and used for the meal that day for the guests and relatives who came to the funeral.

The coffin, which was covered with an embroidered cloth,

was lowered from the men's shoulders. Then the priests began their chanting as they performed the rites for the departed spirit. Presently the rites were ended, and the procession continued to the graveyard. It was a long procession and filled with meaning for the people who took part in it. There were paper models of houses, servants, and carts for the use of the one who died when he got to the unknown world.

After the coffin was lowered into the brick-lined grave, clods of earth were thrown on it, and the paper articles were burned. The rite was intended to drive off the evil spirits.

The next few nights I found it difficult to sleep. I could still hear the doleful music, the horrible death wails of the family and friends. I could still see those pagan rites, undertaken in pathetic desperation to provide the deceased with a few comforts for the unknown world and to keep the evil spirits away. There was no comforting presence or hope such as that which I had known when my father went to be with the Lord.

5

On our first trip to the villages I was disturbed by the physical needs of the people and the lack of doctors and medicine. There were herb doctors and those skilled in acupuncture, which attempted to heal disease by sticking needles into various parts of the body. And every village had its midwife to help with the delivery of babies. But there were few doctors such as those I was accustomed to. I was disturbed as I saw the illnesses that took lives because there was no Western medicine available, and the communicable diseases that so often swept like ravaging fires from one village to another.

"Isn't there something I can do?" I asked a young doctor who was passing through our city on his way back to America.

"You can do a lot of things."

For the next three days before his sailing he gave me an intense briefing on the most common symptoms and the medicine I should administer to combat those illnesses.

"Just don't touch anything that isn't dealt with in the notes," he cautioned, "and you won't get into trouble."

He need not have been concerned about that. I was determined to do what I could to treat the people in the villages where we were going, but I recognized my responsibility, my own limitations, and the seriousness of what I was doing. Constantly I asked God to protect me and the people who so trustingly placed themselves in my hands.

For as many hours of the day as I had the time and strength, there were always patients waiting to see me. Our eye treatment was especially needed and effective. With God's help, I was able to administer the medicine that effected cures which amazed the people and brought even more to see me. Although I turned away many when ailments were too complicated for my feeble knowledge, I did not cause the death of any of the patients!

My "medical" activity gave me contact with many non-Christians and those who did not come to the classes at the church. I hoped my helping them physically would demonstrate His compassion for them—that actions would take the place of words.

On one occasion a wrinkled old lady watched the makeshift clinic for a time after her own eyes had been treated.

"Why do you do it?" she asked curiously. "What do *you* get out of it?"

I used her questions as an opportunity to witness.

"God loves everyone," I said. "He loves you. He wants to enter your heart to live and help ease your pain and suffering."

The look in her eyes revealed that she did not understand. The Chinese Christians continued to talk to her, filling in the gaps left by my poor grasp of the language. They told her about Jesus Christ and His dying on the cross so she could be saved. They pleaded with her to respond to His love, but she was still unable to grasp what they said.

"But what do *you* get out of it?" she demanded of me a second time.

Miss Leu explained it to me. "It is hard for her to understand that you aren't being paid for what you're doing as Chinese traveling medicine men are. The people she knows are only concerned about themselves and their own families. She can't grasp that you can care for her, a stranger, enough to want to help her."

The old woman left and I thought that ended the matter, but she came back in a few minutes, her hands tucked up her long sleeves. She laid six eggs on the table.

"Here, I want you to have these. I can't stand to have you get nothing out of it."

I thanked her. "But you don't have to do that. I'm happy to share Christ's love to me with you."

I thought perhaps she would leave again, but she stayed for a long time, watching and listening.

"I hope you will accept God's free, unearned gift," I told her as she left. "We can't pay Him for that love."

That night we talked about the "egg lady," as we called her.

"No, we cannot earn Christ's love," Miss Leu reminded us. "Nor does our service make us deserve it."

"His love must flow through us to others," Miss Heng added, "if we love Him."

*   *   *

New music was an unexpected added facet to our ministry. Until then, the singing at our services had been the translated familiar hymns of America and England. It was a satisfying type of music for the missionary but was often bewildering to the nationals. Sharps and flats were hard for some, complicating the unfamiliar group singing that the church had introduced to China. Such music gave a foreign quality to the service that constantly reminded some that Christianity was, somehow, Western. It was an invisible barrier for many.

The new music was Chinese in orgin and tone. Verses and

42

entire sections of the Bible, and especially the Psalms, were set to ancient Chinese tunes. They were easy for the Chinese to sing and Miss Leu led the congregational singing, going over and over the songs until they were singing enthusiastically and joyously.

I'm afraid I was still something of a curiosity when I undertook to go back to the headquarters city without my co-workers. I broke the two-day bus trip by stopping at night in a town where two indifferent Christians lived. Whether they had found the attraction of sin too strong or had buckled under persecution, I was unable to learn, but they didn't seem to care about the things of God. They did welcome me, however, and one, a former teacher, reluctantly arranged for a meeting that evening in the large, empty ancestral temple.

When we got there we found that curiosity had brought out a standing-room-only crowd. Everyone who could get in had come to see the American woman who was going to speak at the ancestral hall.

No long scrolls bearing the ancestors' names, and no soul tablets that were ordinarily put up for their worship services and holy days, were in sight.

It was my first attempt to meet a large group of non-Christians without my co-workers. The indifferent teacher and the cook who accompanied me both spoke briefly of Christ. God gave me a freedom I had not had before in speaking, and the crowd evidently understood what I was saying because they did not leave. Of course it could have been that they were curious to see "the foreigner."

"We will come back here some day," I promised them as the bus left the next morning, "and stay here for a while to teach you more about Jesus Christ."

Later, after a number of months and visits to many other villages, Miss Leu, Miss Heng, and I were on the same road again—this time by wheelbarrow. It had been a long trip and we had gotten off the barrows several times to walk, change places, and rest our aching leg muscles. We *did* thank God for our wheelbarrow.

The teacher, who had been so indifferent before, had become interested since my visit and urged us to come back. He even offered us the use of the extra house in his courtyard for the ten days we would be there. As soon as we arrived, he and his wife invited us in for supper.

"Bandits have been around again," our host said as we sat at the table, "taking people for ransom."

That was not surprising to us. It was well known that bandits roamed the area, and at night we had often heard the three shots fired which signaled that someone had been taken for ransom. When that happened I would tuck the bed covers a bit tighter about me, breathe a prayer of gratefulness that we had been spared such a fate, and ask God to have mercy on the captive.

Our host did not continue the subject until we had finished eating. Then he told of an incident that had just happened. A man from a nearby village was terrified when the bandits seized him. He was sure there was no one who could pay the ransom asked and that death was all he could expect.

Suddenly he recalled something strange that he had heard, something that might help him. He couldn't remember who told him or where he had heard it. He was so overwrought that at first he couldn't remember what it was for sure, and his mind wrestled with it.

"Oh, yes!" he said to himself. "I know now. Somebody told me that Jesus is God!"

The joy that glinted in his eyes died as quickly as it came. He didn't even know who Jesus was. But there was no one else for him to turn to, and his heart seemed drawn to this strange one he had heard about.

Kneeling, he prayed aloud, "Jesus, they say You are God. Please help me."

As I heard the story, my heart cried out for the poor man.

He hadn't prayed in Jesus' name. Could God answer his prayer?

But the following day the man was released, unharmed, even though no ransom had been paid. When he got back home he knew where his help had come from. He told his story to a relative who remarked that she had heard of a woman who knew something about this Jesus. So he went to talk to the Christian.

"And that lady, Mrs. Kung, will be here tomorrow so you can meet her," concluded the teacher.

"Will the man come, too?" I asked.

"She will tell him," he replied, "So perhaps he will come."

Alone in our room that night we talked about the strange incident in guarded tones. I was still puzzled, because I knew that God had set down definite rules for prayer, and one rule was that a prayer must be "in Jesus' name."

"Perhaps God was so eager to enter the man's heart that He stepped outside the regular rules," Miss Heng observed. "Don't you think He might do that to enter the tiny crevice that was opening?"

"We understand the rules of prayer the same as you," Miss Leu added, "and we're sure that in most cases you are right. But, in this, we've got to accept the fact that God worked anyway."

"God did enlarge the tiny opening the man's prayer made," Miss Heng concluded. "He went to talk to Mrs. Kung to learn more of Jesus."

Before going to sleep that night, we prayed that the man would come to hear us the following day.

The next morning we met in an empty room across the street, which had been filled with benches to accommodate the people we were expecting. We hadn't started the meeting when the teacher came in, his smile telling us the man had come to the service.

"And the people with him are his neighbors," he explained.

As usual, we began teaching the fundamentals of a meaningful Christian experience. We spoke of God, His love, His revelation in Jesus Christ, and the meaning of the cross.

As long as we were in the village, that man walked from his home three times each day and brought his neighbors with him. The Holy Spirit seemed slowly to enlarge his ever increasing understanding and acceptance. After one of the meetings when we presented the cross carefully in every detail, he came up to us.

"Teachers," he said humbly, "I have never heard any of this before. You say that Jesus Christ died for my sins. But that can't be! Mine are too great! How can He possibly forgive all the wicked things I've done?"

We asked him to wait behind after everyone else had gone so we could talk to him alone.

"No sin is too great to prevent God's forgiveness," we told him. "Christ's love is more powerful than sin. So all you have to do is to kneel down and tell Him frankly and openly that you want His forgiveness for everything you've done. He died for you. He will forgive you."

The man knelt on the floor and made a full commitment of himself to Christ. The joy of his heart shone on his face as he got to his feet.

"I want to tell you about myself." He related the same story the teacher told us, verifying every detail. But there was more, and as he continued, his usually passive face grew animated and even more radiant than before.

"Not long after I was released I became sick and was ill for several weeks. Suddenly one night my room filled with a bright light. A person in a shining white robe that stretched to his ankles stood in the light holding a leaf in his hand. He gave me the leaf and as he did so he said, 'I am Jesus. Take this leaf and it will heal you!' Then he went out of the door and the room was dark again.

"I was healed instantly!"

We could scarcely believe the man's story; but, looking into his eyes, our doubt vanished. It was true. It had to be.

"After that I went to Mrs. Kung. She told me a lot more about Jesus and sent word for me to come here. Now you tell me that Jesus died for me. How can I express my love for Him?"

It was amazing that step by step the Lord had led this man, who had no Christian background, into increased understanding until he surrendered his own will and put his trust in God.

In sharp contrast, one girl from the same village became a Christian after just a few days in the class.

"Suddenly I wanted to believe," she said simply.

So, by dozens of heart-tappings by the Holy Spirit, a church sprang into being and grew up in that village. The old, the young, the literate, and the illiterate came. And the indifferent found a new meaning in life. The teacher who had not seemed to care when we first stopped for the night in his village became the bulwark of the church and the surrounding area. He inherited the land where the building we met in was situated and later gave it for a church. There was no need to meet in the ancestral temple again. Christ had a home in the hearts of the people, and they provided a building for their meetings.

6

*We were on still another church visit by train and wheel-*barrow when we stopped at the home of an elderly widow. The traveling had been hard that day and we were grateful for the opportunity to sit, cross-legged, at the low table on her brick bed, letting the weariness seep from our aching backs and legs.

She prepared eggs for us, broken in boiling water and served in a bowl to drink. Only the very old or the most special of guests were served such a delicacy. We were honored beyond measure.

As we visited after lunch I asked her about the brick pagoda we had passed a few miles down the road. The Chinese were a religious people, and there were temples everywhere—each with its special story.

"We saw a man worshiping there as we came past."

"Ah, yes." Memory twinkled in her sunken eyes. "I know that temple well. I used to worship there."

It all began many years before when a beautiful young girl heard a group of aesthetic Buddhists tell of the way to be assured of future blessings. She became one of them. Miss Lee decided that she was not going to wear the red bridal clothes that were the lot of other girls, but was going to forego marriage and give her life to the aesthetic search for God. She was reaching for Nirvana, the heaven of the Buddhist which is a state of "nothingness," a melting into the universe, as a drop of water in the pool of life.

She was told that evil comes from desire, so any desire is essentially evil. She would have to suppress all thought, and in doing that she would rid herself of desire.

Miss Lee sat on her brick *kang* bed many hours, day and night, practicing deep meditation.

Our hostess paused in her story. "In order to do that, 'five hearts must turn to heaven.'" she explained. "One is the heart of the body, two are the upturned palms of the hands and the two balls of the feet."

Before I could question her, she continued, "You see, the correct way to sit on a *kang* is with one's feet crossed over and turned so the balls of the feet are also turned up. That is the way Miss Lee sat, day after day, trying earnestly to suppress all thought in order to become 'nothing!'"

I could see the poor girl in her bedroom, torturing herself day after day in order to wipe out the last traces of her personality, to become as though she had never been born.

"I, too, was a follower of the same path Miss Lee was trying to walk," our friend told us. "Only I fasted and sat in meditation like she did for a few hours on certain days."

"But why?" I blurted. Such acts seemed so senseless to me.

"We believed that on earth one must suffer out the sin, not only committed in this life, but those in any other former existences we may have had," she explained patiently.

I remembered what another modern aesthetic had said. "If I do evil things in this life, I will become a pig later."

By this process of meditation and starvation, Miss Lee

hoped to avoid some of the inevitable rebirths she would otherwise have to go through to lessen her personality. To her way of thinking, life was so empty, so miserable, that this shortcut to nothingness was worth all it was costing her.

"There is no place for compassion in a religion like that," the older woman went on. "If someone would have tried to help Miss Lee, he would only have been prolonging her agony."

The story continued.

"Miss Lee was very sincere, but one night I heard her say to her disciples, 'I am not finding God. Perhaps I talk too much.' After that she meditated in silence."

Word of her determination to find God by means of silent starvation spread widely in the three years before she died. People came from many villages miles and miles away to worship her. They were worshiping her when she died. Only as death pressed close upon her did she break her silence.

" 'This is not the way to find God,' she said. 'It is dark ahead and I am afraid. Do not follow me. There must be some way to find God. Go and search for another way!' Those were her last words.

"But those of us who followed her could not believe she spoke the truth in her hopelessness. So we took up an offering and built the seven-tiered brick pagoda you saw, and we buried her in it. She died in a sitting position, so we placed her in that position in a large earthen jar. A second earthen jar was turned upside down to cover the top portion of her body, and was cemented to the first. When the coffin was finished, it was shaped like a huge egg. We whitewashed it and painted it with flowers. The seven-tiered pagoda was built around it."

As she spoke I thought of the magnificent marble pagodas in Peking, some of which had fourteen tiers, and the music the wind made whispering through the bells on each point of the tiers. They, too, were built as a burial place for aesthetics like Miss Lee who had spent their lives trying to find the way to God. They, too, housed worshipers who continued to come and pray because they knew nothing else.

"Why did you keep on worshiping there?" I asked.

"We didn't know anything better," she said. "So we came there in hopeless desperation, praying that Miss Lee would help us find God." Her smile winked. "But I am a Christian now."

She went on to tell how she had met a woman on the road from the pagoda who told her about Christ, how He came as a baby and then, as a man, died on the cross.

"She said that if we ask Him, His perfection can cover us as a garment, covering our sin. I had never heard His name before, but I learned that He takes your hand and your sin goes into His heart. He holds the hand of the Father, so He is the bridge to God. Miss Lee worked so hard to find peace, but she never did. I discovered that through Christ I could experience peace in my heart." Her face was radiant, "See what a difference He has made in me!"

I realized again what a privilege it was to be able to tell others of the Lord Jesus Christ who can bring that wonderful peace to their lives.

*   *   *

We had been at a northern village where we were surprised at having fresh crabs from the sea to eat and had been enjoying ourselves immensely. Now, however, it was time to leave.

The weather was hot and harvest was at hand. When the wheat nodded, golden in the wind, waiting for the sickle, and the farmers and their families were working frantically to gather in the grain, there was no time for visiting or trying to hold meetings. The people were putting in long, exhausting hours harvesting the precious crop, and they had neither the time nor the strength for anything else. They loved us, but at harvest they wanted us to leave them alone.

51

For days I had been ill with a serious intestinal upset. My medicine-box remedies, which had helped so many others, were useless. No matter what I did, I was without relief. Therefore I was glad to start home, although I had been dreading the ordeal.

My barrow man fixed the wheelbarrow so I could lie down, and we set off. Out on the road Miss Leu and Miss Heng's barrow men were far ahead. It wasn't long until they left my road for another destination and I was alone. Even our helper had walked on.

Desperation surged over me as I realized the situation, but I was too ill to do anything about it. Frequently I had to ask the impatient barrow man to stop so I could get off and find relief behind one of the many grave mounds that lined the rough road. The condition worsened, and several times the barrow man went on, leaving me to catch up as best I could. More than once I had to stretch out at the side of the road in the sun to rest for a time before gaining the strength to go on.

The barrow men had been reluctant to leave their harvest, but had agreed to take me as far as a certain inn. We left the village at daybreak and were to get to the inn by noon. I would ride a mule to a walled city some distance away where I would spend the night with a teacher friend, and the barrow men would get back to their harvest. The city was so far away that it would have been difficult for me to reach it before the gates were locked for the night, even without delay.

I had no way of knowing what would happen now, and at that moment I was too ill to care. Finally I caught up with the barrow man, who was resting in the shade and stumbled into an inn. I dropped exhausted onto a clean mat-covered bed just inside the door.

Soon our helper came with a bowl of noodles for me. I

looked up at them and shook my head. I couldn't sit up long enough to eat. In a little while he came back.

"You will have to make up your mind. If you are going on, you must go *now*. If you don't, you will have to travel at night and the men won't do that. If you don't go now, the man who is furnishing the mule for you to ride to the city says he is going back home so he can finish his wheat harvest. Say what you will do!"

I had never felt so desolate—so deserted by everyone. I was alone and sick, and I had no idea what to do. I did not even have faith enough to ask God anything specific. I had no plan of my own, not even the words to form a request. On other occasions I had asked God for help, feeling that I could get by somehow, even though He didn't help me. This was different.

"Lord, here I am!" I moaned in utter, helpless surrender.

Immediately, as if a current of electricity went through me, I felt healing and well-being flow into my body. I was well!

Amazed, I sat up, ate the noodles, and rode the mule to the city. That afternoon I sang as I rode. I didn't have to get off once. I could scarcely believe it. Yet, it had happened. Why?

It certainly was not because of my own worthiness or lack of sin. And it wasn't because of my strong, unwavering faith. In honesty I had to admit that my faith that noon at the inn was as unstable as quicksand. Perhaps it wasn't for God's glory for me to be sick and alone in the inn. Once again I learned that God is free to step out of man's preconceived rules.

When we met again I told my Chinese coworkers what had happened. They, too, were astounded at what had taken place. Often one of us had been ill and the others took care or her, but we had never had this experience.

The three of us thought long about it and discussed it a

number of times. We were always trying to figure God out, to try to understand why He did or didn't do certain things.

"Might it be that the deeper we open our hearts to commit our wills, the more God can do to help us?" I asked.

Miss Heng thought one of God's hardest tasks must be to get us to release our own desires. "I think we would like to decide what we want and what God's highest love for us will be," she said. "But no one can do that. We can't get God to work for our own selfish purposes."

"Even Jesus said, 'Not my will but thine be done.'" Miss Leu reminded us.

Everything they said was true. "But, if we can't know ahead of time, what can we do?" I asked. "All we can know for sure then is to surrender in faith to God's highest love and let Him work out our problems in the way He sees fit."

Such trust was not easy, but we were learning to practice it against the time when we would need it far more than we did then.

* * *

After Bible class Miss Leu and I were walking along the beach when we saw a boat standing offshore a hundred feet or so with several men in it. It was a fishing boat and looked as though there was a pile of fish in its middle.

"I wish they would come over here," I remarked. "I'd like to have some fresh fish."

"Maybe I can get their attention." Miss Leu waved to them. "Come on over! We'll buy your fish!"

Instead of doing as she asked, they turned quickly and poled away.

"If I had called to them," I said, "I'd think my Chinese had a relapse."

We thought no more about it until a man burst into the house where we were having supper.

"You have saved our village!"

We stared at him. What could be the reason for his startling cry?

"It's true! You saved us! The men in the boat thought you were officials calling to them. They were fooled by your long garments!"

We understood what he meant about the long clothes. Ordinarily men and women in the village wear short garments for work during the summer unless there was some sort of ceremony. At this time of the year only officials would have on long garments.

"Those men would never dream of women teachers in modern clothes being here, and when you called out and waved, you frightened them."

But we still couldn't see how that could possibly have saved the village from anything.

"We've learned that they were bandits," our visitor went on. "They had a man they had taken for ransom, covered up in the bottom of the boat."

"That's what we saw, and we thought it was fish!" I exclaimed.

"And they were coming to our village to capture someone here until you frightened them away." He drew himself erect. "We certainly thank you."

Once again God had intervened. This time for a pagan village.

7

*I shall never forget the aged priestess we met at the nun-*nery near Weng Chia Tsun. She hobbled to the gate in response to our knock, a spindling, twisted woman leaning heavily on her cane. Her gray hair was thin and scraggly and her eyes sunken by the ravages of the years.

"Won't you come in?" She knew we were not worshipers by our clothes and unbound feet, but she was gracious and kindly. Courteously she led us from shrine to shrine, showing us each of the dust-free idols and explaining the name and the area over which each idol ruled.

"Venerable teacher," I said at last. "You have learned here the way of life, haven't you?"

Her black eyes narrowed and for an instant anger gleamed.

"You have found peace within these temple walls, haven't you?" I persisted.

"Peace?" she screamed at me. "Peace? There is no peace! I have hell waiting for me!"

Shocked by the vehemence that erupted from her, I questioned further.

"How long have you been here?" I asked.

"My mother gave me to the temple when I was five years old."

I knew about such things. The Chinese mother's heart breaks at giving up a baby, of course. It was done only when there was no food. Boys were kept, even in poverty, because they could help to farm the land. And they would carry on the family line and the worship of their ancestors. Girls were another matter; they were expendable. When food or money was scarce, the girls were often given as children, to the temple or sold into prostitution.

The bent arthritic who was showing us through the temple had been dusting those same idols of wood and metal for over seventy years. They were immaculate, even in dusty North China where most things were free from dirt only by comparison. She had been a good high priestess, teaching the girls under her with care and managing the temple land holdings. She was highly respected in the community, known to everyone as a "good" high priestess.

Now she began again, baring her bitter hopelessness to us. "I just depend on the temple for food. Hell is waiting for me."

We told her that need not be true, that there was a way in which she could find forgiveness and her heavenly home. We went on to speak of Jesus and the cross and our holy and just God who loves everyone and has provided a way of escape from the punishment so sure to come.

But she had been too long in the temple. The good news that Jesus Christ died so she could have a new life in Him and an eternal home in heaven was all foreign to her. She had difficulty in understanding it on the first hearing.

We went over the fundamentals of salvation once more, carefully, but her mind seemed as closed as the two doors she shut behind us some minutes later. Standing on the outside we could hear her mournful, haunting wail of fear.

"There is no way!" Her cane began to tap a fierce beat

on the stone walk as she limped painfully back to her room. "There is no way! There is no way!" The memory of her is vivid; we often prayed for the aged priestess.

*　*　*

At another village the room outside our bedroom was packed with people. Benches had been brought in and every available seat was taken. And still they came, crowding in to stand in the corners or anywhere they could find space for their feet. There was no longer a place for me in the room. I was within the adjoining bedroom. Miss Heng was speaking.

"I'll be in here praying for you," I whispered in her ear as she stood in the doorway to begin talking to them.

While she spoke about God's love for them and the Lord Jesus Christ He sent to save them, I knelt on the *kang* and began to pray for those who were hearing His Word. Presently, however, my prayer changed, and I was a little girl at home, for the first time feeling the tug of the mission field. And I hadn't liked it.

At an evening service in the first church I could remember, a lady missionary had been speaking. She had put her hand on my very small head and said, "This little girl would make a good missionary."

On the way home I began to cry. "I don't want to be a missionary," I told my mother.

"You don't have to worry about that, Irene," she comforted. "If God wants you to be a missionary He'll make you *want* to go."

"Are—Are you sure?"

"I'm positive."

Reassured, I began to dry my eyes. God must not want me as a missionary, I decided. I certainly didn't want to go. The truth was I hated the thought of it.

When I was in the seventh or eighth grade I was peeling

potatoes with a long, sharp knife. It slipped and I slashed three fingers almost to the bone. Blood gushed out and I was positive the flow could not be stopped in time to save my life.

"Oh God, don't let me die!" I cried in terror. "I'll be a missionary!"

When I went to Muskingum College the challenge to the mission field kept coming. I listened for a time and was almost persuaded to indicate my decision, but there was a special young man I was interested in who turned my thoughts in a different direction. I was sure he was not interested in being a missionary and was equally sure I could not live without him. I discovered later that I could live without him, but by this time I had shoved the thought of being a missionary back in the dustiest room of my mind where I hoped it would lie, forgotten.

I graduated from college and was teaching in Oregon when God began to speak to me again. This time a missionary made another plea and I reeled under it. I was the only person in the church that night, as far as I was concerned, and everything he said was just for me. Still I did not yield.

I had a good teaching position, I reasoned. It would be foolish for me to go to the mission field when I had everything going the way I wanted it. So I tried to ease my conscience with a good-sized check. The church treasurer was awed by it, but I'm sure it meant nothing to God. Money wasn't what he was asking of me.

In my case revolt came later. After going through college and teaching a few years, I decided I had to get away so I could be free. My father an elder, my sister the pastor's wife, and my traditional background had me hemmed in. I also wanted to go some place where it got cold enough so I could ice skate. I decided to go back to school. And the school had to be inexpensive. So I chose Moody Bible Institute, which my family would certainly approve. How God must have laughed to see me going there—in rebellion.

There was order in the way He dealt with me at Moody, but I didn't see it then. At first I wasn't going to the mission field at all, but I planned to work hard, limit my spending, and give large sums of money to missions. After all, I told myself, that was important, too.

Only God didn't want my money, he wanted me. "Go ye into all the world and preach the gospel," was His reply.

When I saw there was no escaping it, I took another step, with even more reluctance. I was willing to go to the mission field, I decided, but only if I were married. I certainly wasn't going without a husband. I wasn't going to the mission field as an old maid, have to wear funny clothes, and never have any fun.

In my rebellion I cried out against the leading of God. "I'll die if I have to be a missionary!"

But He wasn't through with me yet.

One morning in chapel they sang "Take the dimness of my soul away." Something welled up within me that I could not control. My rebellion against God melted and I quit fighting stubbornly against His will.

All right, God, I said inwardly. *I'll die, then, if that's what You want. I must be in the center of Your will!*

I expected my entire world to collapse because of my deep surrender to Him. And at that moment it would not have mattered if it had. My life found a new center—His will.

And surprisingly to me, mother's remark—in her effort to comfort me when, as a little girl I was crying about going to the mission field—came true. God *had* made me *want* to be a missionary!

So China, that unknown world, sprang into being for me through many circumstances. A whole new life absorbed my attention—the people, the villages, the language study.

Now I had surrendered my will to Christ and had told others about His cross and that He forgave sin, but I had never been aware of the fact that I, personally, had any sin.

I had even read Paul's statement "Christ was made to be sin for us," more times than I could remember. But the fact that it was related to me, did not penetrate very deeply. I had been so respectable and self-righteous and church-oriented that I had never experienced the consciousness of sin in a personal way.

Suddenly, while I was kneeling on the brick bed in the tiny room, I was conscious of Christ's intense suffering on the cross. It was as sharp to my inner self as a sword. I could see Him there! And for the first time I knew that all of His agony was for *me*.

In my inmost being I realized that my years of self-will and rebellion had been hurting God. They were actually sin! It was not so much for outward acts of disobedience. (I had conformed so well to the ways of our family and the church and even the school that they never suspected the truth, but my inner attitudes were very selfish.)

I was now aware how pride, the things I did and said, and my attitude to Mother and to others, separated me from God —and that self-centered alienation was the root of sin. My arrogance and pride had hurt others and in doing that, I had made Christ suffer.

"Oh no!" I cried. "Christ, let me suffer, not You."

I wept.

Deep sorrow and repentance filled me. Into my heart came healing, pardon, peace, and freedom. The forgiving, suffering Father had forgiven. I knew, too, that sin once forgiven, need never be confessed again. It was gone. Wiped out in an instant, and need be wept over no more. Great thankfulness filled my heart.

I was free!

Not free to do as I liked, as when I determined to have my way. But free to become, bit by bit, what Christ wanted me to be. I was a captive slave—perfectly free to become like Christ Himself. Free within the circle of love for the other person as he said at leaving the earth—'you love as I love you'—even to death.

I marveled at His patience in dealing with me to break through my hard self-centered attitude to make me a different person and to bring me to this village in China to work and pray with my co-workers.

*   *   *

The cynical looked at the converts in China and gathered them all together in one scornful phrase. They were "rice" Christians, they said—people who made a profession of walking with Christ to gain favor with the missionary and get something he had. Sometimes it was a bowl of rice given in compassion, or perhaps a few clothes, or the medicine to cure an illness. And I had met that kind during my first years in China. I, too, was disturbed by their pretense. But we had met the other kind, too.

Miss Leu, Miss Heng, and I found such a family in a tiny house on a very small plot of farm land. They had only a little food. When we went into the yard we saw a sick old man, bone thin, lying on a bed of boards. His covering was a single cloth, and his only shade and protection against the elements was a frame of thinly thatched cornstalks above his bed.

Inside, we talked with his daughter-in-law. Her face shone at the mention of Christ and His love.

"You must meet Grandfather," she said, leading us out to greet the old man. His wrinkled face lighted as he told us of the wonders of Jesus Christ and His forgiving grace. He ended with a Chinese phrase, almost slang, that is quite impossible to adequately translate into English. "Jesus is too good to me. There are no words to express how wonderful He is. He is God."

As we walked away Miss Heng spoke in a hushed voice. " 'In Christ ye are rich . . . filled with the fullness of God.' "

'What joy I have in my life with the Lord,' I said, thinking of these people.

*　*　*

In another village Mr. Shan, who was a poor man and a Christian, lived across the path from the house of a rich man who had a baby. Bandits came at night, put a gun to the chest of the Christian and demanded his baby.

"We have no baby," he said. "Search the house, if you wish."

They realized their mistake and still holding the gun on him, demanded to know where the rich man's baby was.

He could have indicated, with a significant movement of his chin, that the baby was in the house opposite his. No words need have been spoken and not even his wife would have known that he had betrayed the child. But the Lord he loved held him true.

"Take me," he said.

There is a saying that bandits never leave empty handed. And it was true in this case, too, for they took him. He had to sell his land and mortgage his tiny home to get himself out of the hands of those men.

Even this costly translation of Christ's love into life did not affect the rich farmer. Feeling himself fortunate, although he knew about the sacrifice, he felt no urge to help.

"I did it all for the Master," Mr. Shan told us, his face radiant.

A Christian friend of ours in the city helped towards the purchase of land for the Shans so they could at least have food.

*　*　*

In another town lived the opium addict, now a new Christian. We were taken to his home where we met him and his wife.

63

"It was agony when the craving came on," he told us. Long ago his home and land had been sold. He and his wife began living in borrowed rooms. His wife sewed and mended to earn a little money for food. But she had to guard even the material she was working on so that he wouldn't sell it for the drug.

"The physical effect—the suffering, the aching of the joints, and the pulling apart of the body all over—is indescribable. It was hell." He told us about those years of being a "dope fiend." His wife agreed that "fiend" was the appropriate word.

The very first time that he heard of Christ he opened his heart in a commitment of faith. Immediately he became a new man and was freed from his intense suffering. "Ye shall receive power," Christ had promised.

No one could deny the reality of his encounter with God. We talked with this man whose happiness was contagious. His body had been ruined, however, by those years of addiction. He lived only a year or two more, then he went to be with the Lord.

* * *
,

An aged teacher came and asked us to visit his town. He had been away from home for many years and had become a Christian in Manchuria. Since returning to his village, he had tried, but could not interest anyone in his family in Jesus Christ. So he came to us and invited us to visit his village and speak to the people. He had made arrangements, he told us, for the meetings to be held in a room in the courtyard of a relative.

There was a good crowd at the first meeting. For no good reason that we could give, we chose the story of the prodigal son as our text. It was not the subject we normally would have used at our first meeting in a village where there were only one or two believers, but it was the text God gave us and the one we used. When the service was over, the wife of the man who owned the house and courtyard where we were holding our meetings came to see us. She was deeply disturbed.

"Who told you about us?" she demanded.

We didn't know what she was talking about. "Nobody said anything to us about you. What is it that we were supposed to have been told?"

"That story you told tonight about the man and his brother. Surely you know the trouble in my husband's family."

We assured her that we didn't. I don't believe she was entirely convinced that we were telling her the truth. The story in the Bible was too much like the one they were involved in. But, making herself comfortable on my *kang,* she explained what had caused her to come to see me.

The seventy-year-old grandfather, a patriarch in the village, had two sons. There was such jealousy and bitter enmity between them that they had not spoken to each other for years; nor had they gone into each other's homes. Their father was deeply troubled by it.

We knew none of this when we came to tell the people about Christ. My coming caused a stir in the village and the younger brother determined that he was going to see "the foreigner."

"I'm not going to let that brother of mine stop me," he told his wife. "I'm going to that meeting even if it is at his house. He won't throw me out with the American there."

He was at the meeting the first day and writhed under God's condemnation of the younger son's evildoing. The older brother's family heard it also, gleefully.

"Maybe this foreigner will show him how wrong he's been," the elder brother whispered to his wife.

When I came to the part in the story about the older one's sin, the roles were reversed. The younger man delighted to hear the older brother also condemned.

The older brother was deeply troubled and puzzled by the portrayal of his own guilt. Surely God couldn't expect him to accept his brother as though nothing had happened between them.

"Go and talk to them," he told his wife. "See if our father or anyone else told her about our differences and asked her to speak on this thing."

That was when she came to me.

The Holy Spirit spoke to the hearts of both brothers so appealingly in the days that followed that they kept coming back to the meetings long after the curiosity at seeing a Westerner should have been gone. Each man sensed his own wrong doing. Each came to pray with us in confession. Each apologized to the other and to their aged father whom they both had mistreated.

That broke his resistance.

The tall, straight, seventy-year-old man also came to pray and give himself to the Master. After we finished praying with him, he pulled out a faded Bible and showed it to me.

"Fifty years ago, when I was a young man, someone gave me this Bible. I don't even remember who it was or why he gave it to me. I put it on the shelf and it's been there for all of those fifty years. I'm not sure anyone ever picked it up. If they did, it wasn't to read." Joy gleamed in his eyes. "Now it has reached my whole family!"

Before we left, the teacher came to thank us for coming. Tears filled his eyes. " 'At-one-ment,' " he said. "Isn't that what *atonement* means? For one to become one with each other and with God. Isn't that the meaning of the word? Now our family has become one with each other and one with God. Thank you."

8

From the first moment I stood on the deck of our passenger liner and watched the picturesque junks move silently across the sprawling Yangtze River and saw the villages rise out of the distance, I had been curious about China. Not the China the foreigner sees—the picture those gracious people showed their guests. I longed to see life as it was lived in the family, inside the high walls and the spirit screens at the gates. I had been living with Miss Leu and Miss Heng, and they told me much about the customs of their people, but that would not be the same as experiencing it myself.

"Isn't there some Chinese home where I can live as a member of the family?" I asked once at headquarters.

"Not that we know of," was the reply.

I had all but given up hope of actually living with the Chinese as one of them when I was informed that I was going to my ancestral home at the next village we were to visit.

I couldn't understand.

"Your Chinese name is the same as that of a woman who lives in the village you are going to," the elder replied.

I had been given a Chinese name by the headmaster of the language school when I first arrived, a complicated process in which he tried to get a Chinese name for me that was as close to my own name as possible. I was given the name Lovely Lotus, A Leann.

I thought little more about it until some time after we reached the village.

As we drew near, an aged woman came out to meet us, leaning heavily on her cane. She had hobbled far from the gate of the walled village to be the first to welcome my co-workers and me. That she was a person of stature in the village was apparent from the way she spoke to us. Her love of Christ was written in her face and in the warmth with which she took my hand.

Etiquette demanded that I first call on her. She took me into the village, leading me by the hand, her fingers tightly clasping mine as though a bond had already sprung up between us. We approached a large brick home with a tile roof thrusting high above the courtyard wall. It contrasted sharply with most of the other homes around it which were made of sun-dried bricks or mud. She took me through a large square wooden gate painted a vivid red and into her living quarters. The rooms were considerably larger than those in most of the homes we stayed in and were well furnished.

She had me sit down and immediately began to tell me about her life, as though I had some special right to know. She was eighty-three years old, the ancestress of a large clan, and a leader in the church. She mentioned those things quietly and without conceit.

She was a Christian now, but the first half of her life she had been searching earnestly to find God and peace of heart.

For years she was drawn, irresistibly, from one temple and shrine to another.

A fly sparked her first doubt as to the power of idols. When she was a little girl there was a fly on the face of the idol she bowed to. When she got up, it was still there.

"If that idol were a god, he wouldn't leave a fly on his face," she reasoned.

She thought about that often but dared not ask her mother about it. She might punish her for such blasphemy. She would have to wait until she was grown up herself, she decided. Then maybe she could find out about such things.

She was over forty years old and had six grown sons when she became eager for a little girl. She did have a daughter and called her Little Precious. The baby was only a few months old when she became very ill; and her mother carried her from shrine to shrine, hoping the baby's plight would incite the pity of the idols and they would cure her. Even the father, who seldom went to temples, walked to a number of distant pagodas seeking help for their baby.

Everyone in the village was worried about Cheng's mother. (In the clan, where all had had the same surname, women were identified by the name of the first child. Her oldest son was named Cheng, so she was known as Cheng's mother.) They knew of her love for Little Precious and feared that if she died, the baby's mother might go insane or take her life.

"I'll carry her with me to this last temple," she said one day. "She's so sick, surely God's heart will be moved to heal her."

On the road she was traveling, a large crowd had gathered to listen to a speaker, a foreigner who spoke of God's love brought to earth by Christ Jesus. She stopped to listen. In all her searching she had never heard anything like this.

If what the stranger said was true, there was more to living than the total destruction of one's personality or being reincarnated in another life as a pig. There was more to the next world than Hell or its alternative, Nirvana, the sinking into nothingness. There was more than the black despair of a hopeless existence.

God had provided a way of escape through the Lord Jesus Christ! Even as she heard those words for the first time she knew they were true and opened her heart to them in accepting belief.

"My baby is sick," she told the missionary. "What shall I do?" There was no doctor or hospital for hundreds of miles.

"Go back home," he said gently. "Ask the heavenly Father to make her well, if He wants you to have her. If He doesn't, He will take her to the heavenly home He has prepared for His children."

She looked down at the baby in her arms. She loved this new God she had just trusted for salvation, but she didn't think she could be separated from Little Precious and go on living.

"You will see her again," the kindly stranger continued. "She will wait for you. Ask the Father to give you peace in your heart."

She did not continue her trip to the temple but went back home, praying as she walked. She hoped the baby would live, and she continually asked God to heal the frail little body; but He had other plans. In a few days Little Precious died.

The neighbors came, grieving, wondering what would happen to Cheng's mother who had been so distraught by her baby's illness. But she was strangely composed. And that they could not understand.

"I'll see her again," she told them, trying to put her new faith into words. "My baby is in the heavenly home."

Their pity went out to her. It was just as they had predicted—grief had stolen her mind!

"Listen to her!" they said. "Who has any idea where the dead have gone? She must be insane!"

They did not know her quietness and assurance that she would again see her little one came from God.

Later they learned that she was beginning to do strange things. She no longer visited the temples and she was praying to a strange God. She even began to go to other villages to meet with people who believed as she did. Their pity turned to distrust.

She was returning from one such trip when her husband's brother met her and hit her in the head with a pickaxe because she was bringing shame to the family by her actions. "That's what you get for listening to those foreign devils!"

She showed me the deep scar that still marred her forehead.

Her mother-in-law persecuted her because she would not prepare the food that was to be offered to the soul tablets of the ancestors.

"But all of that was forty years ago," she told me, smiling.

"And what happened then?"

"My entire family became Christian," she said. "I had a lady teacher come to teach the girls, including those who were engaged to my six sons. She taught them to read the Bible so they could teach their sons and daughters about Christ's love.

"We were very poor, but God blessed us with industrious sons and good crops, and now we have plenty—more than enough."

It was true. God had blessed them with prosperity. It was evident throughout the lovely home.

All of those things she told me the first time we met, as though there was a special bond between us. I was drawn to her from that first enchanting hour or two we spent together. And in the days that followed, I grew to love her even more.

She was happy but all of her life she had longed for the intimate love of a daughter.

I stayed in her home, sleeping in a room adjoining hers.

In the middle of the night I would be awakened to hear her praying for a long list of people by name. There was a deep, loving reverence in her voice as she would say, over and over again, *"wo dee ju"*—"My Lord, my Lord."

And then the news came. When I first heard it, I was sure that there must be some mistake, that people were reading more into a deep friendship than ought to be.

"Have you heard?" one of the younger women said. "Grandmother is going to adopt you!"

"Isn't it wonderful?" someone else exclaimed. "We'll call you aunt or great-aunt or sister."

"Not me," another laughed. "I'll be calling you great-great-aunt."

It was not long until the venerable Chinese woman herself informed me of her decision.

"My only daughter died when I became a Christian. The Heavenly Father has sent you to take her place. Your surname is the same as mine. That makes you more than an adopted daughter. You are my goddaughter."

She did not ask my permission. She was one of those strong personalities who could not conceive opposition to her decisions. After all, she was used to ruling the women in her clan.

She went on to explain that my name would go in her ancestral record, an honor scarcely understandable for a Westerner. She regretted that all of her land was divided among her six sons. She would have liked to have me share in that inheritance. But she did have something for me. Her last undivided possession. It was a beautiful mirror on the wall by her *kang* that had been sent to her by a son who was living in Manchuria.

I could only guess what it meant to her.

"Oh, no!" I exclaimed. "I couldn't take that." I was afraid the others might object.

"Then you won't be my daughter," she said sadly.

What else could I do but accept?

She called her six daughters-in-law and had them wrap the mirror in my bedding. The next day I left, riding on one side of the wheelbarrow while the mirror was on the other.

"I will try to be a good daughter to her to make up for the empty space on the wall."

By taking the mirror I became related to most of the clan living in that large town. I even became great-aunt to Miss Heng, something neither of us could have even dreamed when we first began to work together.

A gift from my adopted mother demanded a gift from me. I had three suits of Chinese clothes made to measurement by a tailor. Our helper made a special trip to my adopted mother's village to deliver the single-layer summer outfit of long trousers and a long blouse, the double-layer outfit for fall, and the thickly padded cotton black suit which would help to soften the bitter January winds. I had shown the proper respect to Grandmother for the honor she placed upon me. Custom had been observed.

But that was not the main purpose in my giving the gifts to her. My own heart was so full at what she had done that it ached. To be loved so much was a humbling experience. I hoped I would in some small way be worthy.

No legal documents were signed to formalize the new relationship. None were required as far as the family was concerned. Grandmother had reached the decision, and she directed the affairs of the female members of the family.

I was one of them. There was no jealousy directed against me. Nothing except love and respect. To have had even the smallest, most thoughtless girl of the clan reject me was unthinkable. They would as soon have rejected their own mothers.

I had prayed for a Chinese home, an open door into the most intimate of family relationships, and God in His mercy answered my prayers in a way that surprised much more experienced missionaries who had never known of this to happen before. I went with my new family through numerous weddings, births, and bitter personality disputes. I grieved with them when there was illness and felt deep personal loss when death came. I knew the joys and the heartaches, the weaknesses and strengths, the secrets that were jealously guarded from the eyes of the outside world. And above all, I experienced the priceless love and unity of spirit reserved for the family's inner circle.

Whenever I opened the medicine box and began to treat the people for their minor ailments, my adopted mother was always with me. She preached to those who were waiting, telling them of the love God has for them and His desire to save them.

"Now you *must* believe in the Lord," she would say earnestly.

There were differences in my Chinese home and my family home in Oregon, to be sure. Adopted-Mother would not throw her arms around me or kiss me when I came. That was not the way of the Chinese. She might take my hand and say, "Oh, I'm so glad you're here." But her eyes spoke more of love than a thousand kisses, and there was adoration in her voice when she talked to me. There was no doubt but that she loved me intensely. Everybody knew it.

And her love of Christ was unequaled anywhere. Often, as we walked along, leaning heavily on her cane and with my hand resting on her arms, she would completely forget that I was there.

"My Lord, my Lord," she would begin to pray aloud, the burden of her heart so overwhelming it cried out to God, "help 'so and so.'"

I was accepted as a member of Adopted-Mother's family by the entire clan, but my acceptance went far beyond that. Christians in other villages heard about it and to them I was no longer a foreigner. "She has been adopted by one of our

74

Chinese Christians," they would say. "She has Chinese background now. She is Chinese."

Like any other daughter, I took every opportunity to stop by my new village home to visit my family. Often when Miss Heng and Miss Leu and I were traveling, we would arrange to stop with Adopted-Mother overnight. It was a joy to be there and a marvelous resting place. We all three looked forward to it.

On one of our stops there I was awakened in the morning by Sixth-sister-in-law's voice outside the window.

"Little sister. Little sister."

Sleepily I opened my eyes and struggled to consciousness.

"Little sister, open the door."

When I did so, she held out her hand.

"Someone gave me an orange. I knew you were coming so I saved it for you."

For weeks I had not had an orange, but I was sure it had been even longer since Sixth-sister-in-law had eaten one. Like David when his trusted aides risked their lives to get him a drink of water from the well of his youth, I didn't want to eat the orange. Yet I knew that it would hurt her deeply if I didn't.

My Chinese home held that kind of love. How could I help responding in the same way? It was as though I were back in Oregon with my own family.

9

In the harsh cold of winter, snow comes often to Adopted-
Mother's village. It came again just before the Chinese New
Year when we stopped for the night on our way to a remote
village we had never before visited. In a brief winter storm,
the drab yellow world was white and shining, the drifts cloak-
ing the ugly countryside with loveliness. At first we thought
we could not go on, but we had twice canceled our visit to
the town we were planning to visit. If we waited, even for a
few days, we would be caught in the New Year's festivities
when it was always impossible to work.

Before the Boxer Rebellion in 1900, when the Empress
Dowager tried to blame the foreign missionaries and Chinese
Christians for China's troubles and thousands of national

believers were killed, there had been a large Christian group in the village we were determined to visit.

Frightened, many recanted when the Boxers came, while others remained true to their faith. Now, years had passed. There were some Christian families whose experience with Christ went back many generations, but the news that reached us was that all were cold and indifferent.

The snow was a hindrance, but we were determined to go on, deserting our wheelbarrows for a tiny, cloth-covered version of a prairie schooner called a Peking cart which was pulled by a mule.

The carter wrapped straw about his legs as high as his knees to keep out the cold as he waded through the drifts beside his mule. We had hot water bottles and a fur-lined rug, but it was still a long, freezing trip.

Near evening the town was in sight when our heavily loaded cart slipped off the road and overturned near the steep bank of a pond. Our belongings were scattered, but we were able to jump free so we were not hurt. Even colder than before, we helped gather up our things and went on. It was after sunset, and darkness was creeping up the mountain slope when we arrived in the town and stopped before the gate of the best-known Christian household. A lad on the street hurried inside to announce our arrival.

We expected the owner of the house to come rushing out and take us inside where it was warm. Any other Christian we knew would have been most solicitous of our welfare. "Are you cold?" they would have asked. "You must be tired and hungry. Come in and sit down by the fire. We'll fix something for you to eat."

The darkness came, and the chill night wind snarled through our heavy clothing and set us to shivering.

"Do you suppose the boy told them we are here?" I asked numbly.

"Of course," Miss Leu replied.

"Maybe they aren't going to come and greet us."

I was about to suggest that we go on to the inn when the door groaned on its hinges, and a dark form stepped out. The stranger surveyed us coldly.

"How long are you going to stay?" he demanded, as though he wished we had not come at all.

I was so startled by his lack of friendliness that I could not reply, leaving the answer to Miss Leu.

"I thought we wrote you about it. We'd like to stay a week or a little longer. We will leave before New Year."

He grunted. "When it snowed we didn't think you would be here. I suppose you'd just as well come in." Because we did not know what else to do, we followed his direction. In the main room of his home he had set up a winepress, no doubt waiting until he was sure our visit would be canceled to begin his wine making. We thought this might be at least part of the reason for our chilling welcome. The making of wine was frowned upon by Chinese Christians even as it is in America.

But we did not comment. The big sin in his life would be his turning away from God and not the fact that he was making wine. The Holy Spirit would have to touch his heart or all our words would be wasted.

We were invited to sit down and the frost began to thaw out of our bones, but their hospitality was still frozen. The members of the family went about their activities as though we were not present. They had obviously had supper themselves earlier in the evening. There was no evidence that there was any preparation of food going on and no one asked us if we had eaten. I turned to our helper.

"Perhaps you had better go to the inn and get some food for us."

When he returned the members of the family watched in silence while we asked the blessing and ate. There seemed to be no embarrassment that we had not been welcomed graciously. We were tolerated by people who wished we would go away. I could not help contrasting our welcome here with the warmth of our welcome in Adopted-Mother's home the night before.

We expected to have an attractive place to meet the next day. Even non-Christians were kindly enough to provide a comfortable house for our meetings, especially in the winter time. But the only available place for our meetings was a house with open eaves and crumbling walls. The wind blew in our faces, and we left our coats on during the meetings, as did those who came to listen.

At this village, it seemed wise for Miss Heng and Miss Leu to do the speaking. They alternated taking the services, informally reading a Scripture verse and talking about it. There was no compromising as far as the women evangelists were concerned. They spoke bluntly of the sin that seemed to have taken hold of the people.

"Long years ago your families had ancestors who were Christian. They took down their god shelves and put away the old ancestral tablets."

The people began to squirm. They knew what was coming and cringed under it.

"What has happened to you after so many years? Have you forgotten your God? Are you grown cold? Have you been praying and going to meetings? And what about sin, the sin of indifference?"

Someone coughed nervously and the speaker waited a moment before going on.

"Have you taken down the ancestral scrolls from their resting place? Have you pulled out the old ancestral tablets and gone back to worshiping your ancestors? Or do you go to the temples to worship the idols men have made? Do you remember that Christ died on the cross for you?"

The message went on, flatly pointing to sin and the need for confession.

"If you feel you have sinned," the speaker asserted, "you must confess. Go over to my companions and pour out your lives."

One by one they came and we would kneel with them on the *kang* while they admitted their sin before almighty God. Sin was confessed and men and women got right with God. Those who had been cold and indifferent when we first began that series of informal meetings were held motionless by the Holy Spirit while the messages were given and came back the next day to hear more. The local school was dismissed so the students could also attend.

We had held many meetings in towns and villages throughout our area in China but we seldom had seen such devotion after God spoke to those hearts. The people sat with their coats and warmest clothes on because the building was so cold, but they did not leave until the service was over and we knew they would be back the next day.

Our host was more disturbed than anyone else, or so it seemed, and he had much more trouble accepting the Word of God as truth. He had been a Christian. There seemed to be no doubt of that. And the people who knew him considered him such. But he had drifted far from God. His experiences in France with a work gang during World War I had been upsetting. Doubts crowded in and he had many questions I tried hard to answer, but he found surrender very difficult. However, the Holy Spirit pled with his heart in a way he could not refuse.

After three or four days of meetings he brought his sin to Christ for forgiveness. The change was dramatic. Although we did not mention it, he emptied the winepress and removed it, and his home became our meeting place. It was more spacious and warm, and the wind didn't blow in. The Christian women vied with each other to prepare our food, and we felt the same fellowship and bond of brotherhood we had experienced with other groups of believers. When our time there came to an end, we were heavyhearted at the thought of leaving.

It snowed heavily again during the day and night before we were to leave, and we considered remaining there until the weather was better, but there were other places beckoning to us; and the Chinese New Year was rapidly approaching which with its festivities would effectively stop our work for a time.

The trip we had to make was a long one, even with good weather, so we started long before daylight, punching our way through the deep drifts. Our carter was inexperienced, and the roads were hidden with snow. Not a good situation in that desolate area. We jogged on in the cold and I sat, my head wrapped in a scarf, and my thoughts of the past few days warming me. I was praising God for His forgiving love and the humble, healed, obedient hearts. And, most of all, that I had been privileged to witness it.

Suddenly, to my utter amazement, the most startling event in all of my Christian experience happened. From high in the air, as though there was a choir loft in the clouds, I heard the most exquisite music I had ever had the joy to hear.

It was in Chinese, which was fitting; the music of a great choir accompanied by harps and an assortment of musical instruments. It was indescribably lovely, a swelling chorus that reechoed in my ears.

"What a friend we have in Jesus!" they were singing— the last song we had sung with the believers before leaving the village.

There was a tiny town to our right and some distance away, but the music could not have come from there. The distance was too great for us to have heard it, and besides, we knew that village well. There was not even one Christian who lived inside its walls. But the music had not come from any place on the ground. The sound was high in the air. It had an other-worldly tone, as though it was too holy to have been produced by man.

"Did you hear that?" I asked my companions.

They hadn't—neither of them. "Hear what?" they asked me.

The music was continuing and I described it to them. The next minutes are etched indelibly on my memory, inscribed on the tablets of my heart with heavenly chisels and a hammer lovingly wielded by God. It was a strange occasion, made stranger still by the music that continued for a time and the conversation of my companions.

I saw the village wall as we skirted it and heard the hushed voices of my companions as clearly as though I was devoting all of my attention to them. At the same time, I was hearing the music and wondering about it. Most of the words faded into the heavenly harmony, but three sentences of one verse were sharp in memory.

"Are you weak and bearing burdens?" one line demanded. "Jesus is dependable as the mountain." And "Why not pray more?" Those lines echoed through my consciousness with trumpet-clarity—commanding, unforgettable. Then, as abruptly as it had begun, it stopped.

There had to be some purpose for it, I reasoned. God must be preparing me for something. But what? I had no answer to that ringing question as we ploughed on through the deep snow.

Some time later we met a man on the path as we entered his village.

"Where are you going?"

We told him.

"Then why didn't you start early?"

Another man, less surly, led us out of the town to be sure we got on the right road. In the afternoon one of the mules went lame, and we got off frequently to wade in the snow, lightening the load in the cart. Early in the afternoon we lost the road and didn't know what we were going to do before the carter located the right direction and finally headed across the fields to intercept the road again.

Through it all I had never been so light in spirit, so unafraid. Hours passed and we were still not even close to our destination. The sun was finishing its course across the sky and lingered red on the distant horizon, as though reluctant to leave us so far from where we were going.

On and on we jounced in the darkening night. It was long after nine o'clock when we reached my Chinese home and Miss Heng's mother, Third-sister-in-law, opened the outer gate after hearing our voices.

"Where *did* you come from?" she cried. "And why are you so late?"

With the bandits around, no one ever traveled at night in that part of China, and especially women. We had never done it ourselves, either before or since.

The purpose of the angels' song? I could not know, but at least we had been kept unafraid and guided over impossible places. My concept of God kept being stretched by experiences. Jesus called us "friends"—could He sometimes want to surprise us with a loving token of friendship? Maybe He has, many times; and perhaps we only call it luck.

The injunction to pray more influenced my activity of the next weeks. I did not take the long trip to the headquarters' city as planned. A personal crisis of a member of my Chinese family needed prayer help. Later events showed the results of obedience to that command.

Some months later, news came from the reawakened group of Christians at the "wine press" village. They were building a church for the first time, at great personal sacrifice. Precious jewelry was sold to get money for the church. The men cut the logs for lumber, and the women carried the mud bricks to the building site. They built a place for worship and called a teacher for the small church school. They even put in a bell to ring joyously of the Lord's day.

We again went to teach them and the students of the recently organized school in the new church building. There was no repetition of our former unwelcome arrival. And when we left, we had an experience much like Paul's. The entire group gathered to pray and watch us get on the carts. They cried as they saw us leave.

10

The Chinese New Year, with its lantern festival on the fifteenth day, is the family holiday, the most important in all the year. It is the great Chinese birthday party when everyone adds a year to his age, a time of traditional ancestor worship and gaiety and feasting. The New Year is the time when everyone goes back home if at all possible.

We had been working hard the past months and needed rest and relief from the crowds that made their demands upon us. Miss Leu went to be with her family, and Miss Heng and I went to our home.

I still marveled at the change my acceptance as an adopted daughter made throughout the entire village. Strangers were seldom welcomed into the New Year celebrations and especially white foreigners. Superstition reared its ugly barriers, adding to the natural distrust of strangers and the desire for families to be with their own. It seemed almost miraculous to me that the entire family welcomed me as one of their own.

The Christian group within our family had many educated members and the oldest living ancestress—Adopted-Mother—which gave us a position of importance within the clan. However, Christians were in the minority. We would be taking no part in the shrine worship, although great care was used in teaching obedience to parents and respect for and remembrance of ancestors. I knew one member of the family who was anxious to see ancestor worship firsthand. I had long been intrigued by it.

The worship was wrapped in tradition. Long scrolls bearing the ancestral records were hung on the north wall of the ancestral hall. Soul or spirit tablets bearing the individual names of ancestors were set on the tables with the words *god lord.* There were many bowls of all kinds of food, white loaves of steamed bread, wine, incense, and paper representing money to be burned.

Home shrines were similar. New Year's Eve each family began the celebration in much the same way. All the desired special food was prepared. If there was money enough for it, everyone had new outer garments. If that wasn't possible, their best clothing was washed and starched.

Early New Year's Eve the sound of pounding meat on the chopping boards came from all sides, as the traditional meat-filled dumplings, *chiao tzu,* were made. Firecrackers began to go off before dark and continued all through the night. Sleep on New Year's Eve was unheard of, except for the wee hours of morning.

New Year's Day was the time for ceremonial visits and feasting. Families who could afford meat only once a year would have it on this day. Men dressed in their best long garments and carrying baskets of cakes in their arms walked throughout the village and to other villages calling on nearby relatives.

The basket full of cakes was essential. One could not go without it. In those calls the equality, dignity, and worth of the individual was expressed. There was no question of financial rating or occupation or social position. Man was accepted for what he was.

The hostess would accept the full basket, remove one parcel of cakes, and put in one of her own to return the good wishes. The caller was served tea and cakes before leaving for his next stop, his basket still full.

I had been thinking a great deal about the family shrine and the large one in the ancestral hall and wondered if I would be permitted to take photographs of it. I asked Sixth-sister-in-law if there would be any objection.

"I'll ask the nephew who is responsible for the ancestral land and for preparing the offering this year," she answered.

In due time I was informed that Ming's mother would allow me to photograph her home shrine and our nephew agreed to my taking pictures in the large ancestral temple.

"Did not our Aunt bring her victrola with her? We would enjoy a concert."

I took the pictures while a crowd gathered and my helper played the victrola for them. Thinking about it later, Miss Heng and I could not help laughing. Surely it must have been the first time a victrola shared a place on the table with the ancestral tablets. And certainly it was the first time Christian hymns were played for a crowd in that setting.

*   *   *

We not only observed the Chinese New Year at our home, but we were present for the engagement of my great-niece, Mei-an, "Beautiful Peace." I looked forward to the event with anticipation, anxious to see the difference Christianity made in their marriage customs. The changes were only in worship, I discovered. Western culture had affected them not at all.

Mei-an and her fiancé had not met, nor had their families. They lived in separate towns and attended their respective church schools. Life did not permit wide contacts.

In the traditional manner, the middleman made the introductions and arrangements between the families. They agreed on a dowry gift suitable to the status of both families. The formal engagement was the bringing of that gift and the written wedding agreement.

The dowry in Chinese culture could not be called a bride price. It served a definite purpose in the family or clan system. Only sons in ancient China inherited the family land or wealth in those days. Girls had no part in that inheritance as they would eventually become an integral part of another family. The dowry became the girl's only financial resource. In some cases it was used to finance the cost of the wedding.

In an older time, custom demanded that after the marriage the bride provide for her own clothes and those of her children. So the dowry, with its money and bolts of cloth, were the bride's future bank account. This sum, never large to begin with, was often not sufficient to meet all of the future needs.

In actual practice the dowry caused a great deal of sorrow. If the families were poor and the dowry small, trouble could come. Often the bride's mother would be so sensitive about the size of her daughter's dowry and her needs and those of her children that she would secretly help her as long as she lived. Such secrets were no better kept in China than they would be in America. Inevitably her own daughters-in-law would find out and resent it bitterly.

Miss Heng and Miss Leu, knowing the trouble the dowry could cause and feeling it wasn't completely Christian, constantly urged a change. They asked Christians to promise in the engagement agreement to provide for the needs of the bride, and especially to clothe their grandchildren. Some accepted this reform. Others did not.

Mei-an's middleman had included the providing for the bride and her children in the engagement, but in this case both families were fairly well-to-do. That meant it would cause no special problems.

It was an exciting day when the men sent by Chen Shan's family arrived carrying the dowry gifts in fitted trays in a framework swung on a pole from their shoulders. Proudly the men entered the courtyard and put down their loads. Mei-an's father escorted them to another room to have tea and cakes. Mei-an's mother served a big meal before the men returned to their own village.

Seldom have I seen such frenzied bustling as the women of Mei-an's family opened the trays, exclaiming over the bolts of cloth—silk suitable for the wedding, figured and plain rayons, and practical cottons in blues and whites. There was the jewelry gift—rings, earrings and hair ornaments of blue kingfisher feathers so beautiful that Mei-an squealed with delight. And there was the money gift wrapped in red paper. Red was the happy color—the color for weddings.

The wedding agreement was in a special tray. Chen Shan's and Mei-an's names and the dates and vows were beautifully written in Chinese characters on a gold-lettered document.

"Let's see the steamed loaves of bread!" Mei-an's mother said, going to the trays that contained them. There were fifty round loaves of white bread about seven inches across. For the women, they were the status symbol.

Wheat was the cash crop and saved to sell. Ordinary bread was made of corn, millet, and *kaoliang* flour, similar to our cornbread. Only on rare occasions such as this was wheat used to make bread.

Knowing she would be judged by the quality of those wheat loaves, Chen Shan's mother had ground the wheat carefully and sifted the flour. Very probably she asked a neighbor whose skill she respected to come in and help. It took great skill to get the brick *kang* bed warmed properly to raise so many loaves exactly right. And when that was done, they had to be steamed in the small, inconvenient, iron kettle stoves. In the winter it was even more difficult.

It was no wonder the ladies were so interested in the skill represented. If the loaves were very white, light, large, and round they were of the highest class. They became the "face" status, or reputation of the family, of the new "relatives-to-be." Neighbors all came to see them, to admire or scorn, making mental notes of this first evidence of what the new family was like, even before they met them.

"There is a smiling loaf," one called out.

I went over to look. Often, if the yeast is good and the loaf well raised, it may crack in the steaming. They are called laughing or "happy" loaves. It was an omen that the marriage would be happy.

Mei-an cut the loaves in slices or in halves to give to the relatives and friends. The thickness of the slice depended on the closeness of the relationship. These delicious slices of bread were Mei-an's "engraved wedding invitations." She gave whole loaves to Adopted-Mother who was her great-grandmother, and to me.

I promised to return for the wedding.

11

As the months and years passed, my heart was growing deeper into village life. I found sleeping on the hard, brick platform bed was good. For some reason even the fleas did not bite me. Miss Leu observed that was because they were Chinese fleas and did not like the foreign flavor. Our food, most of which was Chinese, was eaten with chopsticks and spoons. I spoke only Chinese and for weeks at a time I saw only Chinese people. What was more important, I was able to make myself understood.

Being so well accepted in the village of Adopted-Mother made going to strange villages in remote areas more difficult by contrast. Even though I wore Chinese clothes and by this time spoke the language with some degree of fluency, I was the strange one, the queer foreigner who came to visit them.

The fact that a sponsoring family invited us to the village and provided us with a place to live while we were there did nothing to dispel the curiosity. Numbers of people walked miles just to look at me, the greatest crowds coming on Chinese holidays and festivals.

When they came, I would find an elevated place to stand or sit so they could all get an easy view. The sooner that was over, the sooner the meeting could begin. I would stand on the dirt piled against the tree trunk, on a low wall, or perhaps on a chair on top of a table. Taking this chance to witness, I carried my guitar and sang a few choruses in Chinese while the ordeal was going on. Some years later the phonograph with hymn recordings replaced the guitar. We always prayed that a word or two of some song might sink into a heart.

My hair was prematurely white, something that was uncommon even among the aged Chinese, causing them to guess my age at a hundred. And they were shocked by the size of my feet, accustomed to bound ones on a woman.

"Like a man's!" I heard them say in disgust.

Even Miss Leu and Miss Heng, whose feet, while unbound, were very small, came in for some of the same open, yet friendly inspections. I'm sure it was more difficult for them to be studied with such curiosity than it was for me.

"She's got a funny high nose and washed-out blue eyes," they would say. And then, because they like white skin, they would usually conclude, "But isn't she beautiful?"

That part I didn't find difficult at all. Imagine being a missionary and being called beautiful! It was the sort of thing that didn't happen in America.

While it was good to get the people to come for any reason, those motivated by curiosity soon quit coming once they had seen what a foreign woman looks like. In those remote, untouched villages the parable Jesus used of the seed and the sower was enacted many times.

During the first days of meetings in a new village, the gospel seeds were widely sown and some fell by the wayside. The hearts of the people were indifferent and unprepared, and they soon went on their way. The number who specifically confessed belief was often discouragingly small compared to the great crowds who heard.

But that was not the only problem. We often sowed in stony soil. So many times one of the younger brides would be so touched by the service that she would come to see us afterwards. "It's so wonderful! I'm going to believe!"

We soon learned not to be too excited when that happened. Too many times they would attend for several days, then we would see them no more. The mother-in-law had learned of it and ordered her to stay away. The root that was not yet deep was torn up by the first show of opposition.

The cares of the world, we found, often choked the seed. Life was too hard for some of the women to listen and their burden was too great. There were too many mouths to feed with too little to do it properly. Water had to be carried from distant wells. Dirty clothes had to be beaten with a stick on a rock beside the pool. The heavy grindstone had to be pulled, if there was no donkey, to prepare the meal or the flour.

We also saw the deceitfulness of riches. The people who had land, enough food to eat, an ox to turn the mill and sons and grandsons which could make a man one of the respected elders of the town—this could also keep him from Christ.

"What else do I need?" such a man would say. And there was no stirring him.

However, there were always those who were interested, who returned day after day to hear the gospel. Often someone we hadn't even known was seriously listening would offer an empty room, and others would loan a bench or two that we might have a place inside to hold our meetings.

In the fall we often held services on the threshing floor when the moon was full and hung like a giant orange lantern in the sky. It made me recall my first full moon in the Orient. I had landed in Japan and was having my first ricksha ride as I looked out on a strange world that included Mt. Fujiyama's matchless beauty. I was weary and felt disconnected from earth and home. After boarding the train I saw the first Oriental full moon slowly come up. What a surge of peace washed over me. It connected me with home. Moonlight preaching in China always seemed to magnify the feeling that ours is one world and that I wasn't so far from home.

The balmy air was welcome after the heat of summer, and the villagers were reaping the fruits of their labors. It was a time of relaxation and enjoyment. Some brought mats, stools, or benches, but most sat on the ground. A table with the lantern and victrola was in the center.

For a couple of hours there was the simple presentation of God and Christ, with singing and Bible stories. After some time, a few timidly joined in the songs, following Miss Leu and the Bible memorization.

I often first broke the barrier of strangeness and watched the reactions to "You are important," "God loves you," "Open your heart to Him," and "He will forgive all sins."

To us the concept of God's love is commonplace, but it is dynamite to a person truly ready and hearing it for the first time.

The Chinese word for love carries the human heart in the middle. Each person is in the center of God's heart of love. God suffers until He can be the center of everyone in the world. Real love—that's it!

To watch some strained, weary face in the moonlight, first incredulous, become alive, relax, accept that love, then see peace break through for the first time took away all of the weariness of the long wheelbarrow road. Life's meaning deepened.

* * *

We found that the "footprints of God" as we called them, struck a responsive chord in the hearts of our listeners regardless of position, wealth, or education.

The first was the surety of some great power controlling

the seasons, the growing things, the changing star pictures in the sky, even life and death. The Chinese symbol of God even points to this. To picture the Supreme Power there is a character representing a field with the lines going beyond the field at top and bottom, touching the dim unknown. To the left is written the character "to worship" which means to bow or worship the Power beyond the field.

Their idea of God is not the same as ours. They think of Him as unknown, far off, sometimes benevolent, indifferent most of the time, but the unpredictable, final authority. One of the old proverbs says, "Heaven does not need a knife to kill you."

We were able to start with their own concept of God, fitting Jesus into it.

The second footprint is a universal sense of sin. All men have a conscience and feel guilt when it is violated. It may be hardened or warped, but it is there and eventually speaks. The Chinese character for sin is written with a fishnet on the top and "wrong things" below, which means "caught in a net by the wrong things."

The Chinese, with their philosophers and great teachers through the centuries, have gone to great lengths to get rid of guilt feelings and avoid the effects of sin. They make vows, give gifts, say many specified prayers with set ceremonies, turn prayer wheels, do ceremonial dances, mutilate their bodies, starve or even burn themselves, and perform good deeds to store up merit or cancel the sin already pulled up against them. Often, if one temple or practice does not seem effective, men may try another.

The Chinese (like many of us) usually finds it incredible that Jesus Christ freely forgives the sin of anyone who will bow and ask for it. His thinking is so conditioned in the opposite direction he finds it hard to believe that forgiveness of sin can be so simple.

There is another Chinese word, so amazing one feels that

God, in His great love for the Chinese people, guided the scholars unconsciously to write it the way they do. The character is made up of a cross (十) with a man (人) on it. There is also a man on each side (大大). It suggests a picture of the crucifixion. But it had been written that way centuries before Christ came. Amazingly the word is *come*.

He takes all of man's sin into his very soul so He can forgive sin. All one needs to do is to *come* unto Him. Like a bridge, he brings the sinner in touch with God who loves him.

The third footprint is that man has an inborn sense of immortality. There is a realization that the real person does not die when the body stops. Ancestor worship is the Chinese attempt to provide a link between the living and the dead. Christ knew that man could not perfect his existence or find satisfaction and freedom from sin in his own efforts. He knew that man alone could not touch the Holy One. Since that first communion with God was broken by man's choice, Christ came to the cross to restore it. But man still chooses to accept or reject the cross.

The way Christ's revelation always fit so perfectly into those basic beliefs always reminded me of another Chinese expression: *shen* is the word for God, and *gee* is the word for footprints. Put together, they form *Shen Gee*, God's footprints, which means "miracle." These three concepts—the sense of a supreme power, the sense of sin, and the surety of death, felt by every human being—are the footprints of God left in each personality. God comes in Christ to stand in these footprints. He loves, He forgives, and He leads to a place prepared. This is the miracle of miracles.

Those three footprints, latent in every man, gave us a starting point by which all of the religions we contacted, could be reached. We used them wherever we went.

*   *   *

The New Year was over, but we were still in that period of New Year leisure that lasts about a month. The days were warm and great crowds packed the walled courtyard of an ancestral temple, seeing the foreigner and hearing of Christ for the first time. When the crowds grew less, the meetings were moved to the home of our host.

We hadn't realized the situation when we accepted the invitation to come to the new village. We didn't know that our host was also an outsider, a foreigner without relatives or other connections there. He bought the land openly when it was put up for sale without regard for tradition or custom. Even though he had paid cash for it, the former owner was furious that his ancestral land was being farmed by a stranger.

As if that was not enough, he had invited a new group called 'Christians' to come to the village and hold meetings and there was an American woman with them. We knew none of this before we reached the village, but it is unlikely that our knowing it would have changed our plans. It was an opportunity to speak for Christ.

At the time of the New Year the Chinese celebrated what was known as the Dragon Festival and the Lantern Festival. Men in costumes, with false faces, gaily carried the cloth dragon for the writhing dances in the streets. Others were on stilts.

They customarily stopped at the home of some well-known person, calling him to come out. It was as if they were honoring that individual by giving him a chance to present entertainment for his neighbors. In return the honored one gave a money gift to the troupe to be used as they wished.

On one occasion while we were in that village the dragon dancers honored me by calling me out to watch their performance and give them the tip. Someone told me later that many people heard the angry landlord curse me openly as I went out. Of course I did not know that, nor did I know that formerly the man had been a bandit leader.

Each night non-Christians crowded into our host's large center room. The door was always kept open. One night the cook, entering late, felt a sudden chill and closed the two panels of the outer door. Almost immediately the former bandit threw a homemade bomb made from a milk can with shrapnel and gunpowder. It landed in front of our door. The explosion shook the house, filled the room with smoke, and shattered the paper windows, but we were all safe. The pigs, a donkey, and a bird in a cage out in the small courtyard were untouched.

It seemed a miracle that no one was hurt. We were especially grateful that the non-Christians were uninjured.

What to do next was of great concern to us. We tried to see the local official the following day, but he would not talk to us.

"It won't matter so much if one of us is hurt," I said, "but what if some of the non-Christians should be blinded or killed? Our work here would be destroyed."

"The new Constitution of China guarantees religious liberty," Miss Heng replied, "so we are within our legal rights. He can't stop us."

I thought about that. "Remember the line in the Angels' song," I told my companions. " 'Jesus is dependable as a mountain.' He wants us to bring the gospel to the people who live here. He will not allow us to be forced out."

The next day we went to see the county magistrate.

"I'm sorry," he said, his indifference showing through the frayed edges of his cordiality. "But I'm afraid there is nothing I can do about the matter. It's not the sort of thing I deal with."

"We are within our constitutional rights," I continued.

"I'm sorry, but I can't give you any more time. I'm really very busy." A new note of hardness crept into his voice.

I knew he was trying to get rid of me as quickly as possible but I wasn't ready to go yet.

"I was at a tea for Madame Chiang Kai-shek when she visited our headquarters' city and—"

His eyes widened and there was a catch in his voice. "You know the Madame?" he asked.

"I've met her. I had a personal talk with her at the tea. She thanked me for the work the missionaries had done and said, 'Christ is the only hope for China.' "

That information was an electric shock to the uncooperative official. He got to his feet and came quickly around the desk, agitation evident in his face.

"You know Madame Chiang Kai-shek," he repeated, as though he could not believe that such a terrible calamity had befallen him. He had crossed the wife of China's leader by being uncooperative with her foreign friend. What terrible thing would happen to him now? "I'm sorry I was not more helpful. Please forgive me. You are right. Our new constitution assures everyone the right to worship God as he pleases. I will see to it that there is no more of this trouble."

"Thank you." I was really not surprised. I had seen God open closed doors so many times.

"Won't you please sit down and go over the facts with me again? I will guarantee your safety and that of any believers in the village. You can be sure of that."

We learned later that before noon he sought out the former bandit and ordered him to leave us alone.

"Why did you do such a thing?" he demanded. "This lady knows Madame Chiang Kai-shek. What if she goes to the generalissimo about it? We'll all be in big trouble!"

Before supper that night the former bandit solicitously came and invited Miss Heng, Miss Leu, and me to his home, making a great pretense of having changed his ways. He had borrowed a Bible, opened it, and placed it ceremoniously on the table with candles at each side.

"I just want you to know," he said, "that I'm interested in becoming a Christian myself."

We talked with him, but we were not fooled. He had no real interest in Christ. He only wanted to make it appear that he did.

Before we left he turned to Miss Heng. "Remember, we are all nationals. We're all Chinese. We live on the same continent. You had better speak well for me."

She did not answer him and he seemed greatly disturbed. "All right." With that he walked home with us.

A short time later one of the Chinese church leaders went to that village and talked with the magistrate. He called the bandit in and made him put his fingerprints to an agreement saying he would not molest any Christians, either nationals or foreign. It was a much stronger document than one attested by a seal.

Later yet, we returned to meet with the small group of interested inquirers. Our former bandit leader heard about our impending visit and informed the villagers that he had gone to a nearby city and registered all his family in the Catholic Church.

"Now I have a foreigner on my side, too."

We didn't believe that he had ever seen a priest, but there were no more bombs.

*　　*　　*

Mr. Shin was an artist-scholar, a man who, in the old days of the Emperor, had been trained as a member of the ruling class. He would have been a governor of a province or a high official had there not been a change in the government. His opportunity to rule was gone but his education remained.

We met Mr. Shin when we made yet another trip to a "first-time" village. Mrs. Wang introduced us to his wife first, who was her neighbor. Mrs. Wang's parents had been Christians, but when she was married and thrust into a totally non-Christian environment she outwardly became just like the others. A short time before, she had gone to visit her minister-brother's church and had come back to God. She was the one who invited us to come to live in her home so we could explain her new joy to her neighbors.

Again there were the curious first crowds; but some sincere hearts, already prepared and waiting, were within them. A number of boys ten to twelve years old started coming to our meetings, which were held twice a day. One day before class, one of the men came in laughing.

"I was just talking with a friend on the street," he said. "He told me he's glad for our meetings. They give his leeks a chance to grow."

The leader of a gang of neighborhood boys had been stealing the man's leeks. Now he was coming to the meetings twice a day and didn't have time to pick them. Before we left the likable lad made his decision for Christ.

One day Mr. Shin came alone to see me after the meeting. He was dressed in his official robe.

"May I see the worthy teacher, please?"

It was our last day to be there, but still I was surprised to see him so dressed.

"All my life I have longed for peace of heart, Worthy Teacher," he said after sitting down. "I have read every word of non-Christian philosophy. There is nothing in any of it to bring peace to the heart of man."

He paused and I waited for him to continue.

"I had always felt that there must be a *way*—some other way. Once, going to market, a man from a nearby village and I began a conversation. I was talking about this to him. 'I have heard there is a Jesus Way,' he told me. But that was all he knew. Now you have come and have brought us Christ. Now I know that God is love. Through Christ I have found the long-sought peace and forgiveness in my heart, through this Christ's cross. Only today I read Jesus' words, 'I am the way, the truth, and the life. No man cometh to the Father but by me.' I understand that and believe it from my experience."

He arose and bowed with great dignity. "I thank you."

It filled me with great joy to hear such an outstanding, highly educated gentleman speak of loving our God, but I was still disturbed by his wife's penetrating question a few days before.

She had come to our room before the morning class to pray about some problem and to talk with us about the things that happened in her non-Christian life, weeping bitterly. "I didn't respect my mother-in-law," she said. "I envied my sister-in-law. I told lies and stole." She stopped suddenly. "It was all so terrible, I see now. But we didn't understand then. That wouldn't have happened if we had been Christians."

She turned to me, stopped by a new thought. "Why weren't we told before?" she demanded. "Why did Christians wait so long to come and tell us?"

That simple question burned into my heart. I had to ask that dear woman's forgiveness.

"I'm sorry, Mrs. Shin," I said, my mind going back to the long, hard task God had, bringing me to the place where I was willing to be a missionary. I was still awed at His patience to have gotten me there at all. "I delayed several years by being unwilling to be a missionary."

12

Going back to my Chinese home as often as time and our itinerary permitted was as precious as ever to me. I found the same strength in my Chinese mother's love for God as ever, the same gentle pull towards greater devotion to our Saviour by her selfless example. I looked forward to each visit with the same eagerness, the same expectancy. Perhaps even more than before, because I saw in her a creeping frailty, as though the strength of her lovely body was at last beginning to crumble.

It was not apparent in what she said, nor in any complaining she might have voiced so we would pity her. The weakening showed in other ways, in the almost imperceptible sagging of her shoulders and the weariness in her eyes.

I noticed it for some time before I became aware of the fact that it was actually true. That night sleep fled from me, as I thought back over our relationship.

She had always been close to God—far closer than I, but now the difference was so much more obvious, as though she were living in two worlds. Her hold on this life was beginning to slip; yet I saw no indication that she was disturbed by it. There was a glow about her, bright expectancy that she would soon be with her beloved Lord. In some ways I had the impression that she was already there, that she had crossed the gulf in one firm stride and had only to lift the remaining foot and draw it across the crevice of death.

When I first came to the village a number of years before, I had been awakened at night by her prayers for her family and friends. Now, as we were walking in the courtyard I saw that she often slipped into prayer.

Prayer with her was as simple and natural as breathing. It was her way of life. "Lord, bless our nephew and bring him and his bride to Yourself," she would say. She was moving even more slowly than before and leaned more heavily on her cane as she found it harder to get around. "Lord, bless my family."

She wanted me with her as much as possible when I was in the village. She insisted upon it. But there were times when she did not seem to want to talk with me. Her conversation on those occasions was with God. It seemed as though she wanted me to share the joy and fellowship she had with Christ.

And how I treasured those times with her.

She did not complain when I had to leave, though I was sure she would have preferred to have me with her. She was aware that I had to be about our Father's business. She would have it no other way. Yet, how her eyes brightened when I went in to see her, or we walked together.

I don't say that to my own credit. God had forged a bond between us.

One day we stopped there, returning from another village. She was so weak and ill she was confined to bed. I was not surprised, for I had seen her condition steadily grow worse over the past months.

"Sit here," Third-sister-in-law said, getting quickly to her feet and indicating the favored position near my sick Adopted-Mother's head. I was to sit on the *kang* in the place reserved for the daughter.

Recognition came to those tired, sunken eyes, tenderly, on the wings of love. Only with effort was I able to control my tears until I was alone in my own room. My own mother was still living, but I felt no less grief than I did later when word came that my mother had passed away in Oregon. The bond Christ built had chains of steel.

I had only planned on staying a short time, a night or two, but I could not leave while she was so ill.

Even while they cared for her, preparations were going on for her eventual death and burial. They were done quietly and in good taste, but things were being readied.

I had not even thought about the fact that custom dictated I would need clothes for mourning until Sixth-sister-in-law mentioned it.

"We will have to have white clothing for our little sister," she said. So they made a long white garment of unbleached muslin for me and cut the white cloth headdress that were the symbols of sorrow in China.

As in most areas of life, Chinese customs were specific to the most minute detail about the amount of white the mourners were to wear. All relatives and close friends wore white garments, but only the shoes of a surviving husband or wife and the sons or daughters were completely covered with white cloth. For the more distant relatives the shoes were only partially covered. They were starting to work on my shoes when Miss Heng's mother, Third-sister-in-law, who was the thoughtful one and who had been given the responsibility for the special care of their mother-in-law, recalled that my own mother was still alive in America.

"If she knew about the white shoes," she said, "It might cause her unhappiness, as though we are forgetting about her and claiming little sister as our own. I think it would be best to leave several inches of the heels uncovered as a sign that we know she is little sister's mother, too."

I could see now why they wanted her to take care of my Chinese mother. I should have known it before. I had seen her weep when someone was rude to the senior ancestress or spoke disrespectfully of her. She had the uncanny ability to scnsc the nccds of others and their sensitivity. (And her daughter, Miss Heng, had also this ability.)

I am certain mother would have understood about the shoes and would not have been disturbed, but Third-sister-in-law's thoughtfulness to a woman she had never met touched me as few things have.

The differences between a pagan funeral and that of a Christian were startling. Seeing my Chinese mother's funeral service, I again thanked God for the freedom believers have in Christ, the freedom from the burden of superstition with which the non-Christians in China have surrounded their death rites. I was thankful for the joy of knowing there is a place prepared in heaven for those who have gone to be with Him.

The white clothing had neither superstitious or religious significance, just as the now-going-out-of-style black for mourning in the western world is only custom. The thickness of the wooden coffin and the brick-lined grave were in direct relation to the family wealth. There the similarities ceased.

Non-Christians bought packs of spirit paper for burning, as we in the west might send flowers. The paper was supposed to assure the one who had gone on that he would have a certain amount of money for use in the other world. Christians never burned spirit-paper, so they all brought a sum of money equivalent to the proper amount of paper to the funerals of Christians. The money was given to the family to be used for the funeral costs or other needs.

Neither did Christians make a spirit or soul tablet. A non-

Christian tablet carried the name and two words, *God Lord*. Translating the tablets into English we would say "John Jones, having become God Lord." He was an ancestor now, and life flowed from the ancestors.

These beliefs were very deep. Even those who may have questioned often expressed the uncertainty of that answer to the heart's deep question. "Where do they go?" "What if my mother is cold and hungry?" they would ask themselves. If a son or grandson became a Christian before the older members of the family, that question nagged at their hearts. "Who will care for me after I am dead?"

The Christians did not prepare bowls of food, nor have the priestly chants or ceremonies that made the pagan funerals so haunting. There was no piercing, hopeless wail of death. When Adopted-Mother died, all of her clan who were Christian, knew where she would go. They had placed their trust in the same Christ who had saved her and had prepared a place for her.

Christians prepared a meal for those who came from a distance and had a time when they read from the Bible and prayed together. Usually they liked to have a minister, if there was one available, or an elder, or even a Christian friend to help with the service.

As I said, the plans were being made and we knew that my Chinese mother would soon slip from us. She was getting weaker, but her mind remained clear and she kept repeating the same phrase over and over. "My Lord, my Lord." Love and devotion still rang in her voice in spite of the closeness of death. As I sat there on her *kang* she kept saying those same loving words.

Then she said clearly to me, "You have been a wonderful daughter. God sent you to me." With that she closed her eyes and stepped into the presence of the living God at the age of ninety-three.

Since she was so old and the highest ancestress for the entire town, there were many white-robed men preceding the coffin. I, in my white robe, walked slowly behind with the women of the family, between the great crowds that lined both sides of the streets.

All along the way I heard repeatedly. "Oh, her American daughter is here."

"Her American daughter came. That is good."

To me she is a precious memory.

13

The great walled city, which we will call Tung Shan, was far to the south, out of our assigned area, a twelve-hour trip on the Yellow Sea. The journey would be long and hard, but it seemed wise to respond to our helper's plea.

"Won't you come to our town?" he had been asking us. "No one has ever been there with the gospel. The people have never heard of Jesus."

We knew something about Tung Shan. It was on the sea and known for its wickedness. Gambling had taken over the lives of the people until it dominated their behavior. There was usually gambling in most places on the Chinese holidays, but the rest of the time there was little evidence of it in public. In Tung Shan the vice had such a hold it was seen everywhere, day after ordinary day even among the women as well as the men.

There was also an open antagonism to the gospel, but we knew little about that. Our helper had asked us to go. We wanted to do so if we could. I talked it over with Miss Heng.

He himself was a new Christian. We were thrilled by his concern for his family and his friends. Other circumstances made the trip seem advisable at this particular time.

The farmers in our area were busy with their crops, and Miss Leu had been called home by an illness in her family. I had finished my yearly Chinese exams so the teacher would not have to go along. Miss Heng and I would make the trip.

We got aboard the small coastal boat and put our bedrolls in a corner of the mat-covered floor of a small room on deck that served as the compartment for first class passengers. Most of the crowd who were traveling on the ancient craft would sleep in the hold, but we paid extra for the luxury of spreading out our bedrolls in surroundings with less stale air.

When the gasoline-powered motor was started and the crew of ten backed the creaking little boat away from the dock, it shook so badly the deck trembled beneath our feet; and I was afraid she would split her seams. Miss Heng and I stared questioningly at each other.

"Do you think we made a mistake getting aboard?"

My companion surveyed the impassive faces of the other passengers. They were relaxed and unconcerned. They would know a lot more about the boat than we would, she reasoned. Most of them had undoubtedly made the trip many times. If they weren't frightened, why should we be?

I can't say that I completely bought her reasoning, but we committed our safety to the Lord and enjoyed the stars that night with our bedrolls out on the deck.

Miss Heng was right, as usual. We made our way to the old city of Tung Shan, the boat showing itself to be seaworthy. We were able to squeeze our way among the fishing junks and find a suitable anchorage.

When we first arrived there were the usual crowds of curiosity seekers; but there were also the rumors, fed by old superstitions and hatred, that hindered us. Christians gouged out the eyes of children to use them to make the foreigners' famous eye medicines. And those two women who pretended to be so good and so interested in everyone? They only used their medicine box and their meetings as a means of hiding their real purpose, which was to lead young girls away to become prostitutes for the soldiers.

In spite of the vicious stories that were told about us, there were those who came to hear us. And among them was "Number One," so named because he was the only son and heir of several families.

He was handsome with mischievous lights in his eyes and a smile as quick as his flashing feet, but he had been built to a shrunken pattern. I had known boys back home, not as small as he by far, who chafed at their lack of size. But not Number One. It seemed not to bother him at all. Neither did it seem to bother him when he was persecuted for attending our meetings. The bully of his neighborhood attacked him and called him "Little Jesus." He told us the story, simply, as though it was really nothing.

"And what did you do?" I asked him.

"I just ran."

He was at every meeting and sat in the light as close to the table as possible, staring at us. I found him most appealing.

By the time the meetings were over, we had a nucleus for what was later to become a staunch group of believers. But, as far as our ministry was concerned, it was unique. Most of the number were children, a few were teenagers, and there was one adult, a woman.

The Lord had rewarded our efforts there and we were looking forward to the time when we would be returning.

We would go home by the same boat we came down on, we decided. After all, it had safely made one more trip. It should be good for another. We wouldn't even have to take food along. It was just an overnight trip.

The next morning, however, our plan didn't seem to be quite as easy and free of trouble as we anticipated. A rising wind caught our heavy sampan as the men at the oars fought their way through terrifying breakers that threatened to hurl us back on shore. Beyond the breakers were the swells, huge, undulating mountains of water that lifted us half to heaven and then plunged us half to the bottom of the Yellow Sea, or so it seemed.

The boat we approached was lifting and falling on those same seas. There was no chance to use a gangplank as we did when the bay was calm.

"Jump when they're both at the same height!" the captain shouted out from the boat.

I felt like asking him just when that would be, but he didn't look to be in the mood to answer questions at the moment.

I dare not look at Miss Heng and I was sure she dare not look at me. As it was, I prayed silently and tensed for that dreaded moment.

"Now!"

We leaped as one—surprisingly, landed on both feet. We were on board.

The owner of the boat never did get through the waves on the shore.

We spread our bedrolls on the matting floor of the first class cabin, where we lay flat, wishing the owner of the boat was where we were and we were on shore.

The night was torturous, but at last it was over, and the captain thought he could detect a lessening of the wind. Taking advantage of the brief respite, he hauled anchor and made way to a nearby town where the harbor, like that at Tung Shan, did not provide for docking but was more sheltered. There we dropped anchor and waited.

Not with patience, however.

If the wind had slackened at all, it must have continued to build shortly after we came to a halt. It seemed to both Miss Heng and me that the beleaguered boat was heaving and wrenching over the continuous seas as wildly and as violently as ever. She groaned and cracked as though she were about to split in two. And, before the storm eased, there were times when both of us wished that would happen; when we were sure that anything, even death, would be better than the stench of the ship, the hunger and the queasy nausea of sea-sickness.

Day and night we lurched with that same rolling motion, punctuated regularly by the tooth-chattering jar of the heavy boat against the anchor chain. We lost count of time—even of days. We saw that it was dark, got light, and was dark again.

At first we spurned the boat's food. The ship's cook for the crew worked in a tiny, dirt-encrusted hole, there was no refrigeration, and the flies were everywhere.

"We can't eat that," I said in low tones. "We'd die before morning!"

Miss Heng agreed.

I don't remember when I found the few potatoes in our basket, but I determined to go to the cook's hole to cook them.

"You'll have to be careful," she warned me. "Brace yourself so you won't fall and be sure to hold on to the pan all the time it's on the stove." She was afraid I would be badly burned. And, indeed, that could have happened. Just cooking anything was an accomplishment, the way that kitchen was tossing.

Miss Heng would have gone with me, but she was seasick whenever she got to her feet, even for a few minutes.

I went down to the kitchen and cooked the potatoes, but I came back to Miss Heng exhausted and as black as the cook. I don't suppose we ever devoured potatoes as greedily as we ate those.

As the storm wore on, fresh water became scarce and we were each allowed only one pot per day. For the first time in my life I knew the gnawing agony of hunger that was always with me. One afternoon one of the men roasted some peanuts and shared them with us. They tasted like a gift from heaven.

Our determination not to eat the ship's food weakened slightly with each passing day. The time came when the bitter drive of hunger overcame our noses and sense of cleanliness. By learning when the steamer would be opened and being there, we were able to keep the flies from the meager serving of rice and vegetables we were allotted.

"At least," I told my companion, "We are accomplishing something in the way of sanitation."

*   *   *

Ours wasn't the only boat that was caught in the storm. A large junk with great eyes painted high on the bow anchored beside us. We realized there were others who were undergoing the same miserable ordeal.

It wasn't long until we were intrigued by the activity on board. They set up an altar on the heaving deck and were making offerings to ease the anger of the gods of the sea. They understood nothing about weather and winds. The only logical explanation they could offer for the storm's fury was the continued anger of the powerful sea gods. Because they wanted it to end, they began to make efforts to appease the gods and restore them to good humor.

We saw them bowing, burning incense, and heard their

114

mournful chanting. But that was not all. They made a mock ship from a broom, put on paper sails, and lowered it over the side of the junk with much bowing and the proper rituals, which included the setting off of firecrackers. It was an offering, a substitute for their ship, to the angry spirit causing the storm. They hoped that their action would satisfy him and he would spare them.

But nothing of the kind happened. The wind blew even harder, and we tossed and pitched without respite.

Later we learned that while the storm was bad, it was not bad enough to curtail the operations of the ever-present bandits. They had gone past our low-lying boat to the nearby town on shore and had taken eighteen girls and held them for ransom. We shuddered when we heard it. Both doors of our tiny room were always open. They could have boarded our boat and taken us, and no one would even have known where we were until the storm ended.

About the time we concluded the storm would never end, the wind grew weary of lashing the ocean and retreated to leave a beautiful calm. For twelve days we had been caught in the teeth of a raging storm. Now the ocean lay as flat and unrumpled as the courtyard of my Chinese family's home. Our ship went back for the owner and manager, we took on passengers and made the trip north in the mirrored heat.

Back home, Mission friends, alarmed by the storm and the fact that they had not heard anything from us, had sent out a man with food and medicine to search for us. The gossip that began to circulate the day we boarded the boat had it that a man almost drowned and I was lost someplace in the interior. Both Miss Heng and I assured them that would have been preferable.

14

Later, when we went to visit the Children's Church, as we called our little knot of believers there, we went by land, although it involved a train ride and long hours by wheelbarrow, and included the fording of four rivers. This was to be a new experience for us. We had crossed wide rivers on bridges more times than we could count, but never before had we crossed small ones which lacked bridges and could be forded.

"What of us women?" I asked. "We'll wade the rivers, won't we?"

"Wade the river?" My co-worker was horrified that I would even make such a suggestion. The look on her face plainly revealed that she thought no proper woman would even suggest such a thing. Then I remembered that dignified Chinese women who cared about their reputations did not show their bare feet. "Disgraceful! You get on your barrow man's back, put your arms around his neck, and he will carry you across." To me *that* was disgraceful!

That, I learned, was the proper way for a women to ford a river. As we approached our first stream I couldn't help thinking about it. I didn't consider myself large by American standards, but I knew the barrowman must be approaching the river with certain misgivings. I was much larger than he was. I didn't know exactly how he was going to manage it. I didn't know exactly *how* to get on his back, either, which was more of a problem than my weight. At the river's edge my barrowman squatted with his arms at his side and his hands turned towards the back as stirrups for my knees. I was supposed to give a little hop, get my knees in his hand, and my arms around his neck. I jumped, almost knocking him down, and hung on while he struggled to keep his balance.

As the poor man stumbled into the water, I started to laugh. He groaned and moved deeper into the swirling water. When we reached the middle, tragedy of a sort struck. I hadn't realized it, but the river bottom was mud and my barrow man was stuck in it. He couldn't move either foot. And the harder he worked, the deeper he sank.

I knew it was terribly rude and I tried to control myself, but I couldn't help laughing.

"Don't laugh," he managed, self-pity creeping into his voice. "It only makes things worse."

I knew that even before he spoke and was ashamed of myself, but I could not control myself, thinking of the ridiculous picture we must have made.

The other two barrow men deposited Miss Leu and Miss Heng across the river and came hurrying back. One got on each side and helped my poor barrow man get his feet unstuck. They stayed with him, giving him support until we got across.

"Ai yah," he groaned, putting me down. "I won't carry *her* again."

I couldn't say that I blamed him. I apologized for my

117

laughter and determined it wouldn't happen when the next crossing came.

Eventually we reached river number two, which was wide and shallow. In one way that made things easier. There wouldn't be so much danger of getting stuck in the mud. But I would have to be carried twice as far as before. I was so heavy for them, the extra distance would add measurably to the difficulty.

The second barrow man tried to carry me. He seemed to be stronger than the first, but was less experienced. He didn't know how to properly support my knees, which meant that I had to cling tighter than ever to his neck. We were half across when I became aware of his heavy breathing. At first I didn't know the reason for it, but as he gasped even louder I suddenly realized that I was choking him.

But what could I do? If I let go, I would splash rather unceremoniously into the river. I relaxed my hold as much as possible and he stumbled on to the other side, fighting to breathe despite the stranglehold that was throttling him. Gratefully he put me down and struggled to fill his gasping lungs with air.

When the color came back to his cheeks and he could speak, he turned to his companions. "I'll not carry *her* again, either."

And there were still two more rivers to cross. I wasn't worrying so much about the third river. We still had one barrow man who hadn't carried me. I figured he would get me across the third river somehow. The fourth stream was something else. What if he made the same announcement the other two had made after carrying me?

I would probably have to take off my shoes and expose my feet, ruining my reputation with the men in the party.

By this time we were all thinking about the problem of getting me across the river on the back of the barrow man, and trying to work out a solution. Miss Leu and Miss Heng were not only shorter and lighter than I was, but they were accustomed to hopping up on the barrow men's backs. They could do so without difficulty.

"The trouble is," they decided, "you don't jump high enough."

"If that's all it is," I told them, "there's no problem. One thing I can do is jump."

The third barrow man squatted down. I put my hands on his shoulders and leaped high—all the way over his head.

"Not so high!" they shouted. "Not so high!"

At that moment I was glad I couldn't look into the minds of my companions.

The third barrow man knew the secret of supporting the bulk of my weight with his hands. I jumped lower, got on his back, and we crossed river number three without any more trouble. A shout of approval went up from my companions.

"You," Miss Heng said to the third barrow man, "are elected to carry her over the next river."

* * *

The children were glad to see us when we reached the market town and were eager to have us hold Bible classes again. But first we wanted to learn how they had been doing. We knew the reputation of the town and the opposition of many to the gospel.

The kids had been subjected to a formidable array of scorn and ridicule. And, surprisingly to us, had withstood it well. They were more sincere and firm in what they believed than some adult converts. And they were eager to learn.

We rented a room and decided that Miss Leu should use it as a makeshift classroom and church where she would have regular classes with them. While this was going on, Miss Heng and I would be going to one of the many untouched villages nearby.

We had a wonderful Sunday with the children, but the service hadn't even started when I realized there was something wrong. I missed Number One.

"Do you know where he is?" I asked the others.

"Oh, he can't come."

I didn't ask any more. I didn't have to. His parents had decided that they were going to put a stop to this Jesus business.

Later in the day he surprised us by slipping into the place where we were holding the meeting; the same ragged, impish lad as always.

"I'm not supposed to be here," he announced, grinning. "My family has been watching me to keep me away, but I slipped out, anyhow."

There was opposition at home, but it was more deeply rooted than the fear that a family member would bring shame to the clan by turning to the foreigner's religion. His family were all devout ancestor worshipers, but through a strange quirk of fate, he was the only boy in three closely related families. In ancestor worship everyone else in the family looked to the male heir to burn the spirit money and to worship all of the ancestors.

If Number One became a Christian, he would forsake their ways of worship and there would be no one to care for them when they died. There would be no one to burn the paper money which was supposed to provide them with food and clothes and meet their needs out in that dim, unknown "wherever." The line of eternal continuity would be broken and their clan would exist no more. This was the worst calamity that could befall them.

So the little boy was in great trouble.

It wasn't long until the blow fell.

After we had gone, Number One's father caught him in their courtyard at home, hauling him close with a savage jerk.

"You've got to give up believing in this Jesus!" he ordered.

Humanly speaking, we would have excused a boy so frail if he had given lip service to his father's command, rather than risk the full force of his wrath. But not Number One. Jesus Christ had the number one place in his heart.

"I can't do that, Father," he said as respectfully as he knew how. "Jesus lives in my heart. I can't stop believing in the sun. Jesus is just like the sun. I know he is there!"

Angered beyond measure, the father jerked off his only son's small padded winter coat and pants and beat him across the back with a wooden-handled brush.

"Do you still believe" he demanded at last, sure that his son would recant.

But he knew nothing of the hold Christ can get on the yielded heart.

"Yes," Number One muttered, fighting the tears.

His father began the beating again.

"Do you still believe?" he demanded.

"Yes!"

"Then go to your Jesus! You are no son of mine!"

In his fury the small boy's father pushed him out of the courtyard and locked the gate behind him. It was a cold time of year and Number One was naked. Shivering miserably, the boy debated what to do. He could not go to his uncle's. There would only be more beating. The only place of safety he knew was the rented room we were using as a church.

When the woman who lived there saw him naked, she took him into her home and, wrapping him in her quilt, had him lie down on her warm *kang* bed. We looked at his bruised back and could have cried.

"Didn't it hurt terribly?" I asked him.

"It hurt real bad," he told us, "but I said, 'Jesus, You come and hurt me.' After that it wasn't so bad."

Later his mother came with his clothes and took him home.

121

"What will you do, Number One?" we wanted to know.

"They'll watch me so I can't come here any more," he said. "But just wait until I grow awhile."

So the others had their lessons without him, but he was one whose faith we were sure of. He had stood like a mountain against the storm.

* * *

Miss Heng and I were determined to keep as busy as possible while Miss Leu instructed the Children's Church. She taught the children to read the Bible in the new fast phonetic script. We would start out every morning, walking with our helper who carried the victrola. Most of the outlying villages had never had anyone there to preach the gospel before we came.

When we arrived at a town, our helper borrowed a table for the victrola and a bench for us. These he put on an open threshing floor or an empty lot. With the phonograph playing Chinese hymns, we soon had a crowd. After we presented the gospel as clearly as possible, we walked on to the next town where the process was repeated. During our short stay in that area, we were able to bring the name of Jesus Christ to twenty or more villages.

Then our last day arrived. One final trip and we would be leaving. We had waited to go to a large nearby town so we could go there on market day when the crowd would be larger.

We got more than we expected. In addition to market day, there was also the funeral of a wealthy well-known man that had brought people from a considerable distance. The streets were jammed solid.

I turned to my companion. "We aren't going to be able to do the same thing here that we've done in the villages. The crowd's too big."

"But what will we do?"

I had no answer to that question. It seemed to me that there was no effective way of preaching to so many. I had not realized, however, that the matter was already being taken from my control.

Word must have raced through the crowd that a foreigner was there. Suddenly, as though someone had just turned them loose and they were fleeing for their lives, the people surged towards us, running at top speed.

We whirled and ran—all three of us, Miss Heng, our helper, and me! We not only ran, we had to keep running. To have stopped would have been to get run over.

Many of the people caught up with us and ran beside us. Children stumbled and fell and still the crowd charged after us. We ran outside the town and kept running until we came to a tree with a wide, high, firm dirt base. We scrambled up it and stopped, breathing heavily. When we were able to talk again we told them of Jesus Christ who died and rose again so they could have eternal life.

Later, we kept in touch with the Children's Church as long as possible. They were a varied group—some firm, others compromising. One young man found work in the city and we often saw him. He was another Chinese Christian with a radiant face. But war cut off our contact in recent years, so we can only pray for this church.

15

The time came for Mei-an's wedding. I was on my way back to my Chinese home village with a gift suitable for the special whole-loaf invitation I had received. As was true in practically every facet of Chinese life, custom was strong in such matters.

Those who received single slices of the white invitation-bread were only expected to bring small gifts, as distant relatives or casual friends. Those who were close enough to the bride to warrant a half-loaf were given special consideration and were supposed to respond in kind. While those who were close enough and beloved enough by the bride to warrant an entire loaf, were looked to for gifts in keeping with the honor bestowed upon them.

I am sure there were those who had no special feelings for Mei-an and allowed custom and the approval of her family to dictate the size of their wedding gifts. As for me, however, it was not custom, but love that prompted me to choose the gift that was at my feet on the floor of the crowded train, just as love prompted her to give me a whole loaf of bread.

I would go as far as I could by train. From there I would have to hire a cart to take me the rest of the way, where I was to meet Miss Leu and Miss Heng. I hoped I would arrive in time to visit with some of the family before the frenzied prewedding activities occupied all their time.

Going back to my Chinese home was different since Adopted-Mother had gone to be with the Lord. I used to wait expectantly for the dim outline of the village to rise out of the bleak countryside and, as we rumbled closer by wheelbarrow or cart, for the first faint glimpse of her roof. I knew she would be waiting as eagerly as I, although there would be no outward display of emotion. She would be sitting near the window, her cane close by her gnarled fingers. And when she heard the noisy vehicle creaking up the rutted, dusty road, she would come hobbling out to meet me.

No more. God had seen fit to take her home to be with Him. The strongest bond I had with the village was broken—or was it?

There was the eagerness with which I was always greeted by the family when I came, the way I was accepted into every situation. Nothing was hidden from me. Even the girls like Mei-an loved me for myself, and not out of duty to their ancestress.

Going home was different, I decided, but it was still "going home." It would always be so. Sitting on that train as it slowed at my stop, I was as anxious as any wanderer to be back with my own.

I was looking around for a cart to hire for the trip to my village when a stranger came up to me. "Great-Great Aunt," he said. "Are you going home?"

I looked at him. To my knowledge I had never seen him before. If I had, the introduction had been brief and I had forgotten him.

"I have my cart here and I'm going home, too. You can go with me."

125

For an instant, doubt flashed. He could be a bandit. They still roamed the hills. He might be using this device as a means of getting me and holding me for ransom. But no, he had recognized me as a member of his family. He could have been lying; I realized, but there was a certain clarity in his eyes that made me sure he told the truth.

"Thank you. I am honored." And it was an honor to have a distant relative recognize my relationship with his family.

He loaded my things and helped me up on the cart. His mule was strong and the load light so he sat on the cart and drove the docile animal by his calls and taps of his whip, not with lines as we do. We reached the village quickly and safely. I was amused at the alacrity with which he accepted the fee I offered. I was his great-great aunt and he was willing to accept me as such, but that did not stand in the way of his making a bit of money. I would have been untrue to my position if I had not paid him for a service which constituted his livelihood.

Mei-an's wedding was the next day and most of the elaborate preparations were already finished. Even Mei-an was ready.

I don't know exactly what I expected, since this was a Christian wedding, but it differed from the pagan ceremonies I had seen only in those elements that had to do with ancestor and idol worship. There were many facets to the day-long ceremony that began very early in the morning when men carried Mei-an's bridal furniture on their shoulder poles to her new home. There were two tall cupboards, a table, wooden trunk-boxes, and chairs to fill the newly papered room that was to be her new home.

The children were waiting around, curious for the arrival of the groom in the village. It wasn't long until the cry went up. "Here he comes!"

A band gaily led the procession to the gate of Mei-an's parental home, followed by two red-festooned palanquins, or chair seats, carried by a number of men. One contained the birdegroom, Chen Shan, whom the curious villagers had never seen. The other was for Mei-an when she left with him.

The crowd murmured approval as the tall, handsome Chen Shan got out, wearing the traditional long blue silk garment and short black jacket. He would make a proper husband for Mei-an and father many sons.

He had the mark of a gentleman. But that was not surprising to them. One of the most trusted middlemen in the area had arranged the marriage, and Mei-an's father had gone over the matter with care and approved. It would be happy and blessed with children. It was a satisfactory arrangement and they were all happy for this new couple.

But there were still formalities to be observed.

Mei-an's father came out to meet him, gravely. They bowed with the dignity of cultured gentlemen and went into the guest house that had been prepared for the arrival of the groom. Mei-an's mother had prepared a feast and it was time for it to be served to their honored guest. When her husband came out to the kitchen for the tray she rushed over to him.

"You have seen him," she murmured breathessly. "What is he like?" She trusted the middleman, but still Mei-an was her daughter and there was a certain heaviness in her heart.

He nodded. "He seems to be all that was promised."

"But—" How did she put her doubts into words without sounding disobedient?

"He seems very likable."

The comment was simple, but the tone in his voice said more than the words.

Her smile winked. "Thank God."

While Mei-an's father was serving his new son-in-law-to-be, I went to the bride's room. Mei-an was sitting on the *kang.* I had never seen her lovelier. She was wearing the red silk knee-length blouse over a beautifully embroidered

127

and plaited red split skirt. She was wearing the earrings Chen Shan had sent her and the very special blue kingfisher-feather hair ornaments in her shining black hair. Her shoes were red and embroidered like her blouse.

"Let me look at you!"

She stood and turned slowly, a radiant glow about her that seems, somehow, to be reserved for all brides. I asked about the skirt she was wearing.

"It has been in my mother's family for many years," she told me. "She wore it at her wedding and her mother wore it at hers."

And, I learned later, there were others who had worn it as well. It was a piece of clothing that seemed to belong to all the family, but was reserved for weddings. To me, that was a delightful custom.

I would have liked to spend a few minutes alone with Mei-an, but that would have been selfish when there were so many who wanted to see and talk with her. I hadn't been in the room more than a moment or two when someone entered with a red cloth-wrapped parcel.

"Here is the gift from your mother-in-law," she said. "Isn't she generous?"

As though Mei-an hadn't known the gift was coming! It was a custom, lost in antiquity, for the mother-in-law to send her new daughter-in-law-to-be ankle-length padded cotton trousers on her wedding day. They made the plaited satin skirt stand out beautifully. But the gift had a message for Mei-an. "You are sharing our life," they said. "We will care for you."

This from the woman to whom her life would be linked to in obedience for many years to come; the woman she was probably already fearing a little.

If the trousers were thinly padded, tradition said her mother-in-law's disposition was sour and difficult. If they

128

were thick, the mother-in-law was supposed to be gracious and gentle.

It might also represent financial status as well as disposition. But if it were true, Mei-an would have an easy time with Chen's mother. The trousers were so thickly padded they gave her an almost hooped-skirt contour.

Girls were coming and going constantly, chatting about the groom and telling Mei-an what others said about him. She blushed at the mention of his name. Although she was marrying him that day, she still had never seen him. This, too, was traditional.

It was almost time for them to go to the groom's home for the actual wedding ceremony, but there was one more formality to be observed. Some no longer exchanged handkerchiefs as a part of the day's observance, but the one arranging the wedding of Mei-an and Chen Shan elected to include it.

It came from the old custom of carrying things in one's sleeves. If two men were bargaining the price of an animal or article at the market and wanted to keep the negotiating secret, they would put their hands up each other's sleeves and make the sign on the arm of the other person.

In a wedding it meant "I've got you up my sleeve," or "I will keep you in my heart." It was a gay event, lacking the serious overtones of so many of the formalities.

The bride could not exchange handkerchiefs with the groom herself, for that would violate the custom of not seeing him before the actual wedding ceremony. So she chose one of her bridesmaids.

"I'm dressed," one of the girls exclaimed. "Let me do it."

She was probably the girl Mei-an had chosen for the exchange all along. She put her hand up the bride's sleeve and got her handkerchief, which she put in her own sleeve. Then, with Mei-an's father to escort her, she went to Chen Shan's room, exchanged handkerchiefs with him the same way, and came back to the bride.

"There!" she cried in delight when the final transfer was made. "Now you have him up your sleeve!"

At last the feast had ended, and the band was playing. The time for the actual wedding ceremony was at hand. Chen Shan was the first to enter his palanquin. Then Mei-an, her head covered with a red cloth, went to her satin-covered bridal chair. The curtain was closed, and the palanquin was swung up to the men's shoulders and she was carried off to her groom's home, her oldest brother walking beside her chair.

With the exception of her oldest brother, Mei-an's family would not be present for the ceremony. That seemed strange to me, but many of our western marriage customs would have seemed strange to my Chinese family. The ceremony at Chen Shan's would be similar to the one I saw at the first wedding I attended after coming to China, except that there would be no courtyard shrine with its worship ceremony. Instead a pastor or elder or some other Christian would offer prayer after the people were gathered in the courtyard.

The third day after the wedding the couple returned to our village so Chen Shan could meet Mei-an's family. Mei-an still wearing her bridal clothes, had ridden a mule led by Chen Shan, making a great red splash on the dull landscape. I was glad I was still there. I wouldn't have missed it.

16

I began to hear about the new believer in our area after I spoke at the annual meeting of the Chinese Christians there. When I finished, one of the men came up and told me about this one he had so recently learned to know and love.

"He walks miles a day preaching to everyone he meets on the road or at the market. I've never seen anyone so eager to bring Christ to those who don't know Him."

That was wonderful, I replied. It was good to know that there was such a person working in our area. There was so much to be done and so little time to do it. I thought my informant had finished, but he still stood there.

"He has built a church with his own money on his own vacant lot. I myself have been over there to preach for him several Sundays."

"That is marvelous," I murmured. There were some who seemed to be strong in the Lord but drifted away. It was gratifying to learn of one who was standing firm and true to his Christ.

"You must meet him!"

Although I heard about him several times, it was a number of weeks before I had an opportunity to meet him. When I did, his eyes widened and recognition gleamed on his radiant face.

"I know you," he exclaimed.

"I heard you tell of Christ for the first time I ever heard of Him. It was in the ancestral temple *fifteen years ago*," he continued. "The teacher, there, and your helper also spoke."

This was a new insight into the effects of our work. We had held the service he mentioned, but at the time I had not realized anyone had been influenced. Before I could speak, he continued, sensing my surprise.

"What you said has never left me. I've thought about it often, but it was just recently that I decided to follow Christ."

For fifteen years he had carried the message in his heart, pondering what was involved and weighing the cost. Now he was a Christian!

How gracious of God, my coworkers and I decided, to give us this peek into the results of our ministry. It was an encouragement not only to keep forging ahead but to continue to pray for those who heard the gospel yet made no decision for Him.

I think I needed that encouragement for the difficult days that followed, when I again went through a personal crisis.

* * *

Mail from home was always scarce and long in getting through, especially when we spent so many long weeks in the villages. I had schooled myself, deliberately, not to think much about home and family except on those rare occasions when I had mail. That was, no doubt, a carry over from my first year in China when I feared homesickness would be a problem.

In spite of that, one day my mother seemed poignantly

near. I thought about her constantly, through each activity and even the quiet minutes of prayer. I remember wondering about it at the time. It had been years since anything like that had happened. Although it was unexplainable, it was good to feel her so close. Not long after that, we were at another village when a letter caught up with me saying that Mother was ill.

During the morning class and in quiet meditation my thoughts raced. I was not at home when my father died! No! That could not happen to me twice! Self-pity began to take over.

You are no one special! The words came to mind as clearly as though someone had spoken them. *Why do you think it could not happen to you?*

I realized that I had been taking Mother for granted, as though I would always have her. In my heart I had never faced the fact that the time might come when I would not have her. So, deep in my heart, I wholly surrendered her to God's love. Such a deep peace wrapped itself about me that I decided she must be well by this time.

We finished the trip we had been on and went back to my Chinese home with geat expectancy to hold a few days of meetings before the heavy spring farm work began. When we got there, a letter from home was waiting for me.

Mother had gone to the Lord on the very day I sensed her joyous nearness to me. That had been before I even learned she was ill or had surrendered her to God's will. For some reason my family had not cabled as when Father died.

"Ai yah! Ai yah!" That heart-breaking, half-wailing sigh was frequently heard as members of my Chinese family and Christian friends learned of my sorrow. They did not know her, but they knew the sting of death and how my heart must ache. They were mourning because I mourned.

The next Sunday was Easter. As I went to play the organ, the faces that greeted me were somber. Before the pastor spoke, I decided that I would share the letter with the people and speak of Mother. I could still hear the horrible death-wail that had sounded for mothers without Christ. It was so utterly hopeless and contrasted so violently with the Christian assurance of eternal life. I wanted to talk to my Christian friends about our sure hope and the comfort Christ's presence gives.

God's Holy Spirit was present in the meeting that day. Something happened in my grief that was totally apart from me. As I talked of the difference in our Christian belief that Christ had prepared a place for us, a marked change could be felt in the spirit of the meeting.

Our human hearts grieve, but mostly for ourselves. Jesus knows that and does not blame us. He also wept.

But hope lives!

The assurance of a glorious new life for the one who has gone on should also be in our hearts. To be with God is to become like Christ. That is what we were born for.

Life on earth is like a minute compared to eternity. We are to live here in preparation for the life beyond. And so, I told the Chinese Christians, we have only cause for rejoicing. These truths should temper our grief and hurt and give us deep comfort. Non-Christian hopelessness and Christian hope are an eternity apart. We shall see our loved ones who have gone on ahead in Christ, and we shall know and have fellowship with them.

As I shared those thoughts, joy and peace replaced the gloom. I felt it.

To many others there also came a release from their griefs and sorrows. In a spirit of praise, we spontaneously sang a well-known chorus.

"Hallelujah!"

17

The years fled and, as the calls continued to come in for us,
the wheelbarrows still groaned as we went from place to
place. The time came when we were able to see a significant
influence on more than forty of those four thousand untouched villages in our area where we had lived and taught.
We had spoken in countless others, but in those forty-plus
villages there were now small groups of Christians worshiping in newly organized churches. The Lord had worked and
our hearts were glad.

But hard days came upon my beloved China. The Japanese swept into Manchuria in the Sino-Japanese War preceding World War II and poured into the northern provinces.
They were a tightly governed, militaristic nation and threatened to prostrate the great but almost helpless giant that was
China.

The Japanese control over the north was far from complete, however, and the American consulate did not seem to
think it necessary to pull us out of the threatened provinces.

135

"You can continue your work," I was told, "only don't get into trouble."

That is an excellent piece of advice, especially in time of war. Unfortunately the helpful consulate staff member was a bit vague as to how that could be accomplished.

Often, as we were moving from one village to another, the Chinese guerillas on the road directed our barrows to go a different route to avoid meeting the Japanese. Sometimes at night, when weariness overtook us, we slept through alarms and awakened in the morning to find that many in the village had evacuated in the night. Sometimes, in response to warnings we were given, we hid our valuables under the nearest haystack. For more than eight months we were cut off from our home base, caught between the Japanese Regular Army and the Chinese guerrilla lines.

We saw villages bombed and burned, and markets strafed. Through those eight months and more we saw the ruthless hand of war laid heavily on the land.

Life brought a new depth and closeness to Him. Daily we reached out for the promise, "He that dwelleth in the secret place of the most high shall abide under the shadow of the Almighty." Every evening we prayed with the Christian group in the village we were visiting and then slept quietly.

Of course, not all believers were true and strong, and not all were spared death and suffering. But there were stories of His protective hand everywhere.

In one small market city the Christians had been meeting early each morning at the church to pray. The closer the Japanese came to their settlement, the greater their ardor for Christ became. This was true even when the foreign invaders reached the town.

"The guerillas are meeting in the church," the Japanese officers were told. "When the bells ring, you can go there and catch them all."

Moving stealthily by night, the Japanese set up their guns across the small stream that flowed past the church building. The bells were rung and the Christians gathered for the morning prayer, as usual, not suspecting the ambush. When they were all inside, the order to fire was given, and the powerful guns raked the frail building.

Terrified, the Christians rushed outside, just as the waiting Japanese had known they would. To their amazement, however, a bank of fog just a bit higher than a person's head settled over the creek. It was so dense that it sheltered the believers and hid their stealthy movements away from the church and to the safety of the next village. Not one was hurt.

They stopped ringing the bell but continued to meet regularly to thank God for His deliverance. Although they met in the church every morning, the Japanese, strangely, did not attempt to molest them again.

Or, was it so strange?

* * *

In the next village to which we were invited, God was breaking through by means of Mr. Tai, an older, highly respected member of the community. When he heard that the Japanese Army that had sacked Nanking was marching with ruthless efficiency in the direction of his town, he was terrified. Having no Christian background and knowing no one he could turn to, he stood in his courtyard, held up his arms, and looked to heaven for deliverance.

"Oh, Great Grandfather in Heaven, pity us!"

Obediently, as though that prayer caught the commanding general's ear, the army turned in another direction and spared his town.

Awed, he prayed again in thanksgiving. "Oh, Great Grandfather, You answered my prayer."

He had lived for many years and had never before heard of such a thing.

Later, business took him to a nearby city, and unknowingly he followed a forbidden path and found himself captured by Japanese guards. All he could expect was torture and death.

Again he prayed. "Great Grandfather, you heard me once. Please hear me again and deliver me!"

After several hours the guard left, unexplainably. As soon as that happened, a Chinese ran over to him. "Follow me," he whispered. "I'll take you away from here."

Later, when he shared his story with an acquaintance who was a minister, he was told that it was the Lord Jesus Christ who had answered his prayers.

"Didn't you know? He loves you."

"But I have never heard of Him!"

He listened to God's way of salvation eagerly.

"So it was Jesus who heard my prayer!"

He went back home and told his nephew all he had learned.

Not long after that, the nephew broke his bicycle on the way home from market. He had no money with him and knew no one in the nearby villages. Remembering what his uncle had said, he knelt on the road. "Jesus," he said aloud. "My uncle says you are God. Please help me."

It wasn't long after that a man came by and asked him the trouble.

"I run a bicycle shop," he said. "Come with me and I'll fix your machine."

"But I don't have any money with me to pay you."

"That's all right," was the surprising reply. "I'll fix your bicycle. You can pay me next market day."

The nephew was thinking about his prayer. He would have to tell his uncle about this. Perhaps Jesus had heard him, too.

Both Mr. Tai and his nephew were overcome with awe and

wonder. They decided that they both had been helped by Jesus Christ.

When the minister who had talked with the older man made arrangements for us to come and work in that village, Mr. Tai prepared a house and was responsible for us. He listened humbly to every word of the teaching periods. The meetings had been going on for several days when he came into our house while we were getting supper, looking utterly miserable. I thought something terrible must have happened and asked him about it.

"All of my life has been filled with sin just the way you have been talking about," he exclaimed. "Will He ever forgive me?"

"All you have to do is to kneel down and tell Jesus all about it. He died for you. Ask Him to forgive and accept Him in your inner self. That's all you have to do."

When he got to his feet some minutes later, his smiling face was radiant. He had encountered Christ and by that essential act of will had related himself to Jesus Christ as Lord. Something new inside was a reality.

About thirty new believers came to form this new church. One wealthy individual who was known to have bandit connections became a Christian and pushed us on his own wheelbarrow, purposely, down the long main street of the town. He was publicly announcing by this act that he had become a Christian.

We were in still another village when a nicely dressed woman came to see us. "Isn't Jesus wonderful!" she exclaimed. It was obvious by the clothes she was wearing that she did not live in the village. She was there visiting and had come to see us.

"Why do you say that?" I asked her.

"Someone told me that Jesus is God," she replied. "Three times when the Japanese soldiers came to our town, I was afraid and prayed for Jesus to save me. They went into every house but mine." Then, as though we may have missed the significance of what she said, she repeated it. "And that happened three times! Isn't He wonderful!"

"Do you know who Jesus is?" we asked her.

She shook her head sorrowfully. That was all she knew about Him. We then told her of His love, how He died on the cross so there would be a way for her to respond to Him. She listened eagerly with an opening heart.

"Jesus," she prayed again, "I have heard you are God and that you want to save me from sin. Please help me!"

In a brief time she was gone. We never knew her name, where she came from, or where she had gone, but we rejoiced that there was another soul bound for eternity with Him.

"Forgiveness in war time is the deepest test of Christian reality," a friend said to us. Deep scars had been left by the war.

*   *   *

The famous Japanese evangelist Dr. Toyohiko Kagawa came to lead several conferences in China. Christians from all over the province were in attendance. They were eager, yet many had been hurt by the atrocities of the soldiers. Barriers had been formed.

At the opening meeting the hall was full, and the atmosphere was tense. Dr. Kagawa came to the platform, and without words just stood, head bowed in silence for many minutes. The silence deepened over the crowd too.

"You Chinese do not want to hear a Japanese speak," he finally said. "We Christians are too few to direct the policies of my country. Japan is not a Christian country. Can you forgive? Please forgive." The wall of resentment suddenly dissolved and was replaced by a spirit of fellowship.

*   *   *

Pearl Harbor Day, December 7, 1941, found me back in

the city, where I was held under house arrest by the Japanese for a period of six months. We were allowed to walk on the streets from one until three in the afternoon, provided we wore a white armband marked with a black capital A. We weren't allowed to enter another's home nor could people call on us. That was the situation until the Swiss were able to get us passage on the first repatriation ship, the Gripsholm.

We weren't aware of it then, but we had already taken our last wheelbarrow ride. When we returned to China after V-J day, the jeep, truck, and car took over. I must admit, however, to a certain longing whenever I think of working in the villages and the many, many miles we traveled on the cumbersome wheelbarrows.

18

Those of us who were well acquainted with China knew the devastation the long years of war had wrought. In the months just preceding the end of the war, I was sent across the Midwest to explain the physical needs of the Chinese and alert Christians to the help that would be required. Little mail from the Asian mainland had arrived, but it was obvious that the suffering was acute and the need staggering. In addition to my visits, I wrote letters to both churches and friends asking their help in gathering used clothing.

And it poured in by the truckload. The packers estimated we had gathered three tons of it, but when it was all boxed, there were ten tons of good, warm coats and suits and heavy sweaters and dresses. They would be strange clothes to the Chinese, to be sure, and especially in the villages where the people were largely unfamiliar with Western dress, but they were warm. They might keep someone from freezing to death. I didn't realize it at the time, but when they reached China even the crates were used to help build refugee shelters, so great was the need. My heart cried for the people.

My Chinese family had been informed of my return after V-J Day and some members who were especially close to me, met me at the ship. How wonderful it was to see them. Miss Leu brought back the Manchurian mirror given me by my Chinese mother. She was relieved at being able to discharge her responsibility, and I was so happy to have it.

Miss Leu was in the city when I arrived. Miss Heng came later from the interior. She had only one thin suit of clothes and no money.

The Ford truck that had been given to the mission by the family of one of our group was the lifeline to haul coal and food. It was even used as a hearse on occasion and as a car to get us to a few outlying churches we could still reach.

That winter was the coldest of my life. I had some heat, a half ton of coal bought at an exorbitant price, and a small kerosene heater, but still I felt frozen most of the time. Even at that, I was warm compared to the refugees. Their plight was unspeakable, and there were times when I felt as though I ought to give away my coal and kerosene in one burst of generosity and live as they did. The only way I could justify being warmer than they was the fact that I had to be able to keep going if I was to help them.

But gradually conditions began to ease. They were still deplorable. There were those who died of the cold and starvation and of illnesses that could have been cured had help reached them in time, but the black despair began to give way to hope. Once more we began to look forward to spending the bulk of our time presenting Jesus Christ to those who had never heard of Him.

I had never had a car of my own in China until a Christian family in California bought one and shipped it out to me.

The word of its arrival seemed unbelievable. I feared I might be dreaming and would awaken to find the car was only a figment of some deep longing I had never before been aware of; but it was really there, safely on the dock. Miss Heng, Miss Leu, and I looked at it and patted it tenderly, as though it were a baby kitten.

"This is going to be better than a wheelbarrow," Miss Leu said, smiling. We sat in the grey station wagon that was complete with five extra tires and spare parts for every conceivable emergency.

In a way just getting the car into China was something of a minor miracle. Getting a license to import any car into China was supposed to be impossible. Yet, something deep in my heart kept insisting that if God had brought it this far, He would complete the transaction.

"The car is here now?" the head of customs kept repeating. "That is too bad. It will have to go back."

"Since God brought it out here, I believe He can find an honest way for it to be admitted to the country."

He eyed me skeptically. "You'd better pray hard. I can tell you now it's impossible."

The American consul general was just as pessimistic. "We've got several cars held up already for permits," he said, "even though we have been told that official cars would be allowed. However," he went on, "I'll do everything in my power to help."

I continued to plead with the Chinese official in charge, impressing upon him the fact that Chiang Kai-shek had just made an appeal for relief goods of all kinds. "I'm working in relief," I said, "and that is the way the station wagon will be used."

I saw a slight but visible change come over him. "I can't make the decision myself. You understand that?"

I was marshaling my arguments for a final appeal when he went on.

"But I'll tell you what I'll do. I'll wire the facts to the Shanghai office and get a special ruling."

On the days of waiting that followed, I kept busy and tried not to think about the station wagon or what it would mean to our work. Finally the call came from customs. They had a ruling, and I was supposed to appear at their office at the

144

earliest opportunity. I was breathless when I burst through the door.

"Congratulations," the assistant greeted me. "You've been granted your permit!"

There was the usual tangle of red tape to unravel and the duty to pay, but we had been prepared for that. The important thing was that the vehicle could come into China. It was ours to use! How we praised God as we drove home.

Most of our activities were directed towards relief in those chaotic days after the end of the war, but my heart was still in the back country, the villages where I had first started working for God. We had more than we could do in the city, but it wouldn't have been advisable for us even to consider going back to that part of China, as much as we wanted to pick up our ministry where it had been stopped by the Japanese regulars. The area was too close to Communist strongholds and, despite all Chiang Kai-shek's valiant army could do, the guerrilla rebel forces were churning relentlessly over the countryside, gobbling up one village and burning another.

We used to hear about the spirited defense of the Communists that was offered by certain elements in the States who called them agrarian reformers, and we wondered if any of our Chinese Christians were being deceived as well. We rather doubted it. They were close enough to the situation to know that all too often the reforming was done with the knife, gun powder, and the torch, and that they left a bloody trail wherever they went. But we were concerned about the Christians and often wished we could see some of them again.

Then the invitation came to attend the fiftieth anniversary of the church in the village which was entirely Christian, the church we called the "Church of the Miracle." The people had miraculously survived a wild, unprovoked machine-gun attack by the Japanese.

145

We talked with those who were familiar with the area and the present location of the guerrilla forces and decided the risk was slight. All of our mission personnel went in the old, secondhand jeep, just for the day. It was a blessed experience that even now is precious to me. It was as though God had cracked the gates of heaven just enough to allow a bit of His glory to show through and anoint our gathering. That was my last trip to the villages.

*　*　*

Warmth anywhere was a luxury in those days. But on Sundays our chapel was almost warm. The truck made continuous trips over the city to collect refugee Christians for our services in the chapel. As each service ended, another load arrived, and the former group was returned. This process continued all day, with the result that the seats hardly had time to cool off.

Soup kitchens helped many to keep alive. A joint committee representing all churches managed eleven soup kitchens. Every morning early we went to the various soup kitchens to preach. Lines of hundreds of people would be waiting. Each person carried a tin bucket or container to collect his hot scoop of rice. Certainly it was hardly enough for even one person for a day's food, but these people would take their meager portion home to share with others. As they waited in line, they heard the gospel perhaps for the first time.

The Red forces had already taken Peking, and the papers were filled with assurances of religious liberty and protection for all foreigners and property. They had not come to destroy, they shouted. They were going to preserve and build. Theirs would be an orderly, responsible government that no one need fear.

We learned that they meant one thing by such statements, and we interpreted them quite differently, but that realization did not come until later. The first news accounts were calm and ordered, seemingly justifying the broad pronouncements that had been made to a concerned world. Our board in the States had been considering the situation and, while seeing alarming aspects to it, felt not yet justified in ordering us home. They cabled instructions for us to get God's guidance about remaining or returning home.

As we met and considered the matter, a scene in *Quo Vadis* came repeatedly to mind. In fact, I had been thinking often about it in the past few days. Peter was fleeing Roman persecution when he met Christ, who said, "Where are you going, Peter? You are leaving. I will go into Rome and die again."

"Oh no!" Peter answered, "I'll go back to Rome."

So Peter went back to Rome and, according to tradition, when they started to crucify him he asked that he be crucified head down, feeling that he was not worthy to die like Christ.

Now, as we talked about remaining behind or going back to America, that story spoke to me. And, somehow, I knew that I was supposed to stay.

After prayer and a great deal of discussion, we announced our decisions. The men and families felt it wise to leave, at least until they could see exactly what was going to happen. In spite of the new regime's protestations of responsibility, they did not trust it.

At last I became aware that everyone was looking at me. "What about it, Irene?" they asked. "What are you going to do?"

I hesitated, wondering if I had the courage to do what I knew God wanted me to do. When I spoke, however, my voice was even and well controlled.

"You have all made your decisions. Before I give mine, I want to exact a promise from you. I want each of you to promise that you will follow your own guidance regardless of what I do. Is that agreed?"

They all nodded that they would.

"I feel that God wants me to stay here and see what happens to the Christians."

We had all agreed that the situation, while serious, was not critical and that no one need be in a hurry to leave. But we reckoned without God. He moved with stunning speed to sweep the other missionaries out of China.

One family had to leave because of a major emergency operation that had to be performed back in America before a relief ship could arrive. They accompanied the daughter of another couple who was going back to college. In Japan the girl developed polio and her mother and father flew out to be with her.

That removed two families.

Because of the revolution, the American school would not be in operation, so family number three had to leave for another Oriental country where they could educate their four children. The doctor was needed elsewhere, which removed family number four. The imminent arrival of the stork rushed another family away, while yet another missionary took his wife out to Hong Kong, planning to return. That, however, proved to be impossible. He was out and the Chinese would not allow him to come back.

A German who had been a Communist prisoner for years later reported, when he was finally freed and back in Germany, that he had learned from authoritative sources that one of the missionary men had already been given a definite death sentence and would have been executed had he not left when he did.

For some reason God wanted the others out of China. For some reason He wanted me to remain.

It was humbling, later, to learn from a Chinese Christian who had risked a brief trip back to his village that one of the women had asked about me.

"Is *she* still there?" she called quietly to him as he passed by.

The church in that village had been locked by the Communists and the people were forbidden to meet for worship.

"Yes," he said, nodding quickly.

"The people know you are here," he told me. "Even though you can't come and visit them, it gives them courage and comfort to know that you are nearby."

In those days Isaiah 54:10 was my strength. "For the mountains shall depart, and the hills be removed; but my kindness shall not depart from thee."

I wondered what would happen under communist rule. Communism was totally new to me. But I believed then, and still do, that the ultimate test of the use of power—no matter what the form of government—is whether the freedom to worship God and justice still exist.

I wanted to have this new experience, so I stayed.

19

The Communist take-over in our city was as swift as it was efficient. One night when we went to bed, everything was normal. There was no unusual activity, no signs of soldiers fighting. I slept soundly, confident that the next day would be the same, uncertain and filled with rumors, but comparatively quiet. After all, we had been living with the Communist threat for weeks and it had not come into being. There was no reason to think this particular night was any different than the others.

But it was.

When I got up and looked out over the courtyard wall, there were soldiers everywhere, moving quietly up the streets in small groups, their weapons cradled in their arms. There was a cold efficiency about their movements, as though they had done this many times.

The conquest was practically bloodless and so complete that at first I had some difficulty in believing it was true. Could it be that this was a different branch of Chiang Kaishek's army? Even as the thought came, I knew how foolish it was and the chilling reality made itself apparent.

The uniforms were definitely Communist. And, as if that were not evidence enough, red armbands sprouted on the school uniforms of many high schoolers, identifying them as a part of the secret army that had been trained and was waiting for this moment.

What does all of this mean? I asked myself. *What will such men do, now that they have our city so completely in their control?* They were ruthless and capable of anything. Of that, I was already aware.

I noted the time. The newspapers would be on the streets by now. Perhaps they would give a few clues as to the intents and purposes of our conquerors. My helper went out to get a newspaper.

The papers were already giving out the official line. I should have realized that reporters and editors would all have been changed immediately if, indeed, the Communists had not already infiltrated the staff and were waiting for this day to surface.

The editorials and news stories marched to what was becoming a familiar drum. The new regime did not want to oppress anyone, they said. It was the purpose of the government to guarantee freedom of worship. The people were going to be free to express their opinions even though they differed with official policy. They were free to make requests of government agencies and to carry on normal life and business. There were to be no controls on the individual. He would be free to serve the State as best he could.

I had scarcely finished reading the paper when I saw that loudspeakers were being installed on the street corners.

"This is the People's Government," they blared. "We are installing the speakers so you can know what is taking place." The voice was not hysterical or demanding. The time for that was later, after their grip on the people began to tighten.

I'm not sure I was aware of that at the time. What they said sounded so reasonable that, although I still did not trust them, I began to wonder if they would actually oppress the Christians. After all, they were swiftly gaining control of the country. Surely they would be wise enough to see that it would be better not to make any more enemies for themselves than was absolutely necessary. My doubts were still there, but I decided to wait until I saw exactly what happened before making any more quick judgments.

It wasn't long until I met my first Communist in an official capacity. He came to my door and inquired politely if he might come in. He was pleasant and seemed almost apologetic, as though he was reluctant to bother me.

"I have a few questions which I must ask you."

"Of course." I stepped aside and motioned for him to come in. I had a few questions I would have liked to ask him, too, but I didn't think I should.

He wanted to know my name, my age, my citizenship, and my purpose for being in the country. I had the uneasy feeling that he was plowing old ground and knew the answers to his questions even before he asked them, but I tried to be as courteous and as candid as possible. When the form was filled out, he returned it to his black leather bag, stood, tucking the briefcase under his arm, and thanked me.

"We do appreciate your cooperation."

I studied those black eyes. Even though his words were mild, his hostility towards me was evident.

"We may have a few more questions, since you are one of the last of your group still living in this province of the People's Republic of China." And with that he was gone.

I stood with my back to the closed door, my hands clasped, and my eyes closed in prayer. There was nothing the official said that should have alarmed me, yet I was disturbed. I felt that I had been in the very presence of evil and hadn't yet seen where this new government was going.

"Dear God," I prayed aloud. "Be with the Chinese Christians in this hour of trouble." Who knew what terrible things would happen to them before this blight was removed from their nation?

Before the day was out, I was visited by two additional officials of the new regime, each wanting more information. The man at the door would come in courteously when I opened it to him, endow me with a bleak smile that was supposed to make me feel at ease, I imagined, and walked from one room to the other. He looked around in silence, as though he had come for the purpose of making an inspection. Then he would pull out a chair and sit down in the office. The inevitable forms would come out.

"Let's see, you have already furnished us with some information, but our files aren't quite complete."

The questioning began again.

"What was the occupation of your mother's father?"

I dimly remembered him as a farmer.

"And her grandfather?"

At first I thought he was joking. "I don't have the slightest idea."

His gaze was withering. "Please think!"

I tried to remember, but that had been a long while ago and he had died before I was born. I thought he was a farmer, too, but I couldn't say for sure. The official seemed most disturbed because my reply wasn't as firm as he wanted it. He came back to those same questions again and again, asking them in different ways, as though trying to trip me. Somehow, I got through that ordeal and when the next two officials asked nothing more about it, I thought that was the end of the matter; but he returned before the week was up.

"There are some things on your forms that aren't quite clear to us. You told me that your father's father moved twice during his lifetime. Is that correct?"

I was about to reply in the affirmative when I realized that he had moved three times. I corrected him.

"Oh, yes. That's right. He moved three times." He leaned forward and the question stabbed at me. "Why did he move?"

I didn't know.

He asked again.

I was only a child, I told him, when my grandparents moved the last time. I wasn't sure, but it seemed to me that they bought a home and moved from the farm to town.

That didn't satisfy him.

"Didn't you ever hear your parents talk about it? Hadn't you seen a newspaper clipping that told about the move and the reason for it? Hadn't you ever seen it mentioned in an old letter or a diary?"

The questions persisted, one upon the other.

What happened? Why didn't I know? Was I trying to hide something? What reason did my grandfather have for moving? What was the name of the town he lived in? Why did he go there instead of someplace else? How many farms did he own? How many people did he have working for him?

As the interrogation continued, it grew harsh, imperious. It was all I could do to control my temper in the face of those evil eyes and accusative tongue. He must have read my irritation.

"Do you want me to make a note here that you are uncooperative?" he demanded. "Would you like to have it recorded that you are an enemy of the State?"

He did not raise his voice, but that made his words no less ominous. I didn't understand then the full import of what such a notation would mean.

"I'm not an enemy of anyone," I retorted, "and I'm trying my best to be cooperative, but you are insisting on answers I can't give you."

He closed the folder abruptly. "I will be back after you have had a little time to think." His mirthless smile returned to rest coldly on his thin mouth. "Perhaps you will remember better a little later."

154

That was one of the most unpleasant experiences I had in being questioned, and the irritation had been so brief that, in thinking back over it, I began to wonder if I had imagined the harshness in his voice and the hate that glittered in those black eyes. He questioned me again, several times, but that was the only occasion when he showed any sign of being ruffled or upset.

Although I tried to keep from showing my irritation, the endless questioning was annoying. Two or three times each day I could expect official-looking callers who wanted to ask a few questions to fill in the blank places in my file or the file of the Mission.

And the forms! I had no idea how many forms I filled out, or even how many copies they required of each. I began to wonder if they had enough men even to read all the forms they required of the few remaining Americans.

By this time, however, I had learned never to question them or argue with a directive. All we could do was to listen carefully to their instructions and obey. It didn't matter how ridiculous the instructions were or how contradictory. If we were to stay out of trouble, we had to do what we were told. I was beginning to wonder if some of those orders weren't designed to draw us into protesting so they would be able to make an accusation against us. I was extremely careful how I talked with them.

After some weeks, during which the new government spoke loftily of freedom and the rights of the individual, the blow fell.

"Because of the decadent condition of our society and the extent of the reforms necessary," the loudspeakers shouted, "extraordinary measures are being taken immediately. In an unprecedented move this morning, it was decreed that all property in the People's Republic of China will be confiscated immediately and without notice. The government is taking full control of all schools, hospitals, nurseries, and labor

155

unions, as well as private homes and businesses. Neighborhood groups are being organized to assist your government in the orderly transfer of all authority to the State."

I couldn't believe it! It must be a propaganda gimmick, a horrible nightmare from which I would soon awaken. Even the Communists would not make such a god of the State.

But they had.

Each additional day it became even clearer than before. No longer were they careful to use the proper inoffensive language when trying to indoctrinate. The city was now secure, and they could move on to the next phase of their program. They were teaching Communism as a religion. There was no God, their announcers scoffed. The individual differed only from an animal in that he is more clever. There were no individual rights. The desires and needs of each person were nothing. He existed only for the good of the State.

And every day there were streams of dejected men, women, and children shuffling in silence through the streets.

"Who are they?" I asked a trusted Christian.

He eyed me critically. The radio had not yet begun to scream against me so it was all right for him to reply—if he was careful in what he said.

"They are refugees," he said. "They ran away from the People's Army who were in control of their home areas. Now they are being sent back to their homes."

I realized, then, that these were some of the people who we had been feeding and clothing when we first got back to China after the war.

"These people are enemies of the state," the man persisted, although I had asked for no further explanation. He seemed eager to get that remark on record so any nearby informer would know of his loyalty. "They will be properly dealt with when they get home."

I shuddered. I had an idea what that would include.

As far as the Communists were concerned, there were only

two classes of people—friends and enemies. There was no such thing as a passive friend. One's loyalty had to be proved and the way to prove it was to inform on the enemies of the State so they could be punished.

Men and women were being forced to attend Communist indoctrination classes every day, and the secret agents were everywhere. Trucks rumbled through the streets, rounding up several hundred real or alleged enemies of the State each night and hauling them out to be shot. Great lists of those executions were posted on bulletin boards at prominent corners so those who might be wavering in their support would see what could happen to them. The Communists were deliberately creating an aura of terror in the City.

The same thing was going on all over China we were told, as that great, peaceful nation was being whipped to her knees. They were after blind obedience on the part of the people and would not stop until they had achieved it.

20

The subjection of our city continued on schedule. Communist teaching instructors indoctrinated their students and tricked them to inform on their parents.

"Go home and tell your mother what I'm saying," they would insist. "Remember exactly what she says so you can tell me tomorrow."

If the mother's answer sounded as though she might be one of the hated enemies of the State, she and her husband could well be on that night's list of victims.

While the Communists had attacked other groups, savagely, they said little about the church at first. But they could not tolerate a loyalty, even to God, that was greater than the loyalty to the State. There were already Communist listeners in all of the churches to report on what was being said.

I was disturbed, but not entirely surprised, when a Christian man came unobtrusively to my home to show me an article in the morning paper. "They're starting on us now," he said. "We may not be able to hold services much longer."

The reporter was attacking the church because we were doing too little for the "common people."

I handed the paper back to my caller. It was hard to understand why they would take such a position. Throughout the church's long history in China, it had been the *only* agency serving the people with educational, medical, and relief work. Our local church leaders had already planned more conspicuous service programs in order to meet just such criticism. We already had organized literacy and homemaking classes.

Even though everyone was fearful of what might be coming, it was decided that we would have services as long as possible. On Monday morning when the group leaders of the church came to my home to report, there was a feeling of exhilaration.

"Praise God!" one of them cried. "We haven't been arrested yet."

We planned a smallpox vaccination drive in a small rural village, but the government would not permit it.

"The church can't accomplish anything," we were told. "Only the government can do good. Only the government can serve the people."

The first orders to bring the church under subjection were insidious. We were never told that we could not believe in Jesus Christ. The illusion of religious liberty was continued with care. We were, however, ordered to "be patriotic." The church was not to become an instrument of subversion against the rights of the people and the State.

Because of this, church services were limited and could only be held at specified times. No home prayer meeting groups were allowed and pastors were discouraged from calling in the homes. Children were pressured to go to a Communist meeting or nursery, arranged exactly at Sunday school time. Christian doctors and nurses were kept on in their positions. Medical help was scarce and badly needed, but their schedules

159

were unexplainably changed so it was impossible for them to attend church or take part in any of its activities.

War had been declared against the church; a subtle, divisive guerrilla war that broke out in unexpected times and places, a war that was hidden by day and waged insidiously at night.

The church itself was not openly declared to be an enemy. But there were changes designed to insure continued loyalty. A Communist was appointed as the head of the Christian church of China and began to speak for all groups, without giving any the right of dissent. He handed down edicts that forced a fearful obedience on church leaders and members alike. Anyone who dared to differ with his directives was branded as a "spy," or a "running dog of the Imperialists." Freedom of religion came to be defined as "Freedom to persecute."

The church was being made a tool of the state.

"Oh God!" I cried out in agony. "Why do You allow these terrible things to happen to Your children?"

I felt I was experiencing a bit of the suffering of Christ. Home was my office. Affairs still had to be cared for.

"Ping" my pet parakeet was good company. Some time before, a friend had given me two parakeets in a cage, telling me that the male could find his way back if I let him out. It wasn't long until he was all over the house, perching on the cupboard or the back of my chair and mimicking my exact tones.

The time came when he surprised me by returning my morning greeting. "Hello, Ping."

"Oh, you are cute!" I had made no conscious effort to teach him to talk.

"You are cute," he continued, repeating what was always my second sentence to him. "You are cute."

"Well," I told him. "If you are going to talk, I'm going

to teach you to preach in Chinese." So I taught him the words *knee shin Chu* which means "You believe the Lord."

He learned quickly and it wasn't long until he had a third phrase added to his repertoire. He always said them distinctly, together, and in that order. Thinking back, it seems strange that I could find comfort from Ping and his saucy phrases, but I did. Often when I returned from a Communist grilling, shaken and disheartened, he would bring back a smile by talking to me.

I suppose God always has His spokesmen in times of terror and persecution—that there are always those, like the prophets of old, who dare to call the people to repentance. But it is a thrilling and fearful thing to see. Such a man was the evangelist from the south who marched into our city unasked and unannounced, and began to hold hours long meetings four times a day in the largest church in the city. The building was packed for every service. Nonchristians who had previously only had scorn for Jesus Christ were there, and so were the few Americans still left in the city.

The leaders of several Christian groups so exclusive and separatist that they had consistently refused to allow their members to enter another church or pray with other Christians were on the platform day after day. All the city was stirred! Terror had unified the church.

We thanked God for what He was doing, but even as we did so, we knew that the Communists could not permit the meetings to continue much longer. Predictably, they struck, arresting the man of God. By this time I knew the pattern of government so well I could have written the charges against him myself.

He was not charged with preaching the gospel of the Lord Jesus Christ. To have accused him of that would have been to admit to the world that they were oppressing religion. Instead, he was charged with being a spy and the tool of the imperialists. They must have been very much afraid of him.

161

The list of charges was long and formidable. Unexpectedly, my name was connected with that of the evangelist in these allegations.

The comrade in charge of relations with foreigners, who had grilled me so often that I always thought of him as Number One Comrade, called me into his office. I went at the appointed time. I had long since learned that such imperious orders had to be obeyed.

"Did you know the evangelist?" he asked.

"No."

"Did you help him to come here?"

"No."

"Did you give him any money?"

"No."

He paused as though he had suddenly exhausted his questions. But he had one more. He leaned across his desk and shot it out at me.

"Are you praying that we will release him?"

"Yes," I said with a fearlessness that was quite apart from my own strength. "I have been praying that you will release him, but that's not all. I've also been praying for you and for Mao Tse-tung."

An electric shock surged through his body, jerking him erect, and murder flashed in his eyes. "Why do you pray for us?"

"You both have souls," I told him. "I pray that you will open your heart to God, so He can save you and work through you to help the land and the people I love."

He seemed to lose all control—all reason.

"Don't you pray for us!" he shouted, beating the table with both fists. And then, as though I had not heard him, he repeated it again and again. "Don't you pray for us! I forbid it!"

I saw the sudden rage and wondered if I, too, would be thrown in prison or executed. But my time had not yet come.

Number One Comrade was still incensed at me and summarily dismissed me from his office.

I was shaken by the experience, but not as much as he had been. For one brief moment, Number One Comrade had pulled aside the shade to reveal a little corner of his heart. For all of his ruthless power, he was actually afraid of prayer.

That night I had to face up to the matter of prayer for the Communist leaders in a much more personal way. What I had told him was true. I had been praying for him and Mao, but much of my purpose had been selfish. I was praying so they would be converted and the church be spared. Now I saw that I had to pray for them with a different purpose. I had to love them, even while I hated what they were doing, and had to pray for them because I wanted to see them saved. I had to ask myself if I loved them as Christ told us to love—even to the death.

Shortly after my experience in the office of Number One Comrade, a Christian doctor decided he should intervene on behalf of the imprisoned evangelist. While he was not a Communist, he had believed the early report that the government was determined to follow the will of the people and that it was possible to go to them with specific requests. With this in mind he went to the police.

"I have two requests," he told them. "My friend, the evangelist, isn't well. I would like to ask that you let him out of jail and put me in to serve his term."

"We'll answer one of your requests," they told him. "We'll put you in, but we will not let him out."

The evangelist never learned that a friend had sacrificed himself in an effort to save him. No word was ever received of the doctor's release and, much later, it was learned that the evangelist had been killed.

The Communists were not finished with me. They made no further effort to link my name with that of the hated evangelist, but they continued to summon me to their offices or come to my home to continue the grilling.

There was something about the tall, officious Comrade my helper showed into the living room that chilled me. Some of the others had at least made a pretense of friendliness. Not this man. He sat down and launched into his questions with the manner of a prosecuting attorney hard after a damaging admission.

"Why does America give relief to China?" he asked.

Relief work! Most missionaries had had a part in relief work over the years. I explained to him that God is love and that Christ's teaching includes sharing. I told him that Christians are the channels of Christ's compassion. That was the reason for the relief-giving that I knew about.

His anger exploded upon me.

"You think I'm naive enough to swallow that!" He leaped to his feet and began to gesticulate wildly, throwing his arms. "You think you are talking to some ignorant peasant! We know why America sends relief! It is to buy China. You want to control our country!"

He acted as though he might hit me.

"Such God nonsense! You missionaries are all spies for the American government!"

For the first time I heard the charge that I was an American spy. It was not to be the last.

My caller left abruptly. As he stormed out, I bowed my head and prayed for him. I had tried hard to explain why missionaries did relief work, but he had not been able to comprehend it.

Like the other Communists I had come in contact with, he could not understand compassion as a motive for doing anything. There had to be a reason for what we had done—a personal reason. Because they would use an institution such as missions as an instrument of infiltration and subversion, they automatically assumed that the American government

164

was doing the same. Why else would missionaries come? It was impossible to communicate with such an ideology.

I saw that nonunderstanding again when Number One Comrade, who had gotten so furious at the thought that I was praying for him, came out to the house to take an inventory of what I had, to see that I had not acquired or disposed of anything since the last check. My parakeet was loose and startled him by landing on his shoulder.

"Hello, Ping," the parakeet chirped.

Number One Comrade was disturbed. He knew the word for hello. "But, what is Ping?"

"That's his name."

"You are cute." Out came the second sentence.

"What does that mean?" He acted as though he was strong on the trail of some new evidence of imperialism.

I explained what the words meant.

Ping was not ready to stop, however. *"Knee shin Chu,"* he said in clear Chinese. "You believe the Lord."

By this time Number One Comrade was staring at the bird on his shoulder. "I do not believe the Lord," he said to Ping in Chinese. "I do not believe the Lord."

21

I could sense a change in the government's attack against the church for some time before it became apparent in the things they did. The relief work and Western influence, including the efforts of the missionaries, had built up a great reservoir of good will for the United States throughout China. In the Communist mind that was a threat to their rule and had to be destroyed. Until recently they had been consolidating other controls. Now they were moving in force against the church.

When the new summons to the Foreign Office came, I felt a certain apprehension but shook it off. I could not see that this particular encounter was to be any different from earlier ones.

While relaxing in my bath, the words "No weapon formed against thee shall prosper" came to mind. And the meaning to me personally was immediately clear.

I didn't even realize it was a Bible verse at first. But I knew that it applied to that particular day.

I hunted through the concordance until I found it—Isaiah 54:17. "No weapon that is formed against thee shall prosper;

and every tongue that shall rise against thee in judgment thou shalt condemn."

I thanked God for that message of hope and encouragement and tucked it away in my mind. While it did not seem to be particularly pertinent at the moment, and the meeting went well, checking back later, I discovered that this had been the time when plans for my death were being formed.

I thought again of that time, years before, when I had heard the angels' song and the promise, "Jesus, as dependable as a mountain."

New orders were in the newspapers. All missionaries were spies in the pay and control of their government, plotting to make the church the stooge who could turn China over to America. These missionary political agents, the papers said, must be turned over to the government to receive the deserved punishment as "spies."

We knew that they were calling us spies and that we were to be accused, but we knew nothing more. A Chinese friend came to me, curious, during that time. "We hear that we have to accuse you," he said. "What does that mean? Is that a way to help you go home?"

There were other rules. The Chinese Christians were to sever all contact with the missionaries. They were to accept no more funds and were even to cut off social connections. The beloved pastor of our church began the service with the hymn, "Be Not Dismayed Whate'er Betide," after sending word to me that I could not attend church there anymore. I stood close to my window and sang it with them, tears running down my cheeks. "God will take care of you." I sang it to them. "God will take care of *you*."

One Sunday we tried going to a German service. The next day the German pastor came to deliver the word in person. "No Americans may attend the German church services."

Then I went to the Russian Orthodox Church. It was Easter and the music was exquisite. Soon after, the civilian leader of this church was arrested. I was greatly disturbed by this. Was he suspected because an American had been attending his church? I did not go back.

The propaganda program had reached the place of demanding that missionaries be dealt with. And at this time, the details gradually emerged. What happened to each missionary was determined by the local situation, by what procedure would best further Communism. Deportation, in some cases after imprisonment or torture, was interpreted as gracious leniency in sparing such vile spies.

The entire procedure was planned with care.

A huge accusation meeting would serve as a national pattern when it was held in Peking. All the church leaders of high position were ordered to attend. The first criminal indicated was an early translator of English literature into Chinese—a man long dead. Then they moved directly to their real targets. They disgraced and accused all of the missionaries in China in great detail; and a number of Chinese leaders who were better known, were arrested and tried. Then local leaders were ordered to go home and repeat the procedure. The proper way of ridding China of the hated foreigners had been ably demonstrated to them.

One leader who had been at that meeting was almost weeping when he told me about it. "One of those missionaries accused was an old friend of my father's. And I had to vote to imprison him!"

The purge had begun.

*   *   *

It was during the early days of this period, in the lull between planting and harvest, that a wizened elder from one of our village churches came to see me. He had walked many miles from the north to the nearest railway station, carrying his shoulder pole and baskets to keep from attracting attention, and had come into the city to see me. He left his baskets

168

out in the yard and slipped into my back door in an effort to avoid being seen by the ever alert Communist eyes that seemed to be watching my every move those days. He was carrying his Bible, wrapped in black cloth, under his arm.

"I have a message from God for you," he said.

I knew he had traveled far and was weary and hungry, so I had him sit down and asked my helper to get him some cakes and tea. Things were bad, but on that particular day I could admit to no specific concern.

"I know people are afraid to come here," he went on, "but God sent me to tell you five things." As though eager to complete this mission he was so convinced God had sent him upon, he opened his Bible to Isaiah 41:9-13 and read the verses aloud to me.

" 'Thou whom I have taken from the ends of the earth. . . . art my servant: I have chosen thee and not cast thee away. Fear thou not, I am with thee: be not dismayed for I am thy God. I will strengthen thee, yea I will help thee. Yea, I will uphold thee with the right hand of my righteousness. Behold, all they that were incensed against thee shall be ashamed and confounded: they shall be as nothing: and they that strive with thee shall perish . . . for I, the Lord, thy God, will hold thy right hand, saying unto thee . . . ' "

He still had not finished. Closing the worn Bible, he spoke again, the tone of authority ringing in his voice.

"The five things I have to tell you are *from God,*" he emphasized, counting them off on his fingers, decisively. "One, tell the people in America not to be too discouraged about the Chinese church. Two, tell them their gifts and offerings have been accepted by God. Three, the church in China will go through great persecution and a time of winnowing the chaff from the wheat. Four, the church will come back in great revival."

Then he turned more directly to me and used, for the Chinese, a most unusual gesture. Ordinarily, in gesturing to

169

someone, they will use their entire hand in pointing, rather than our direct, blunt forefinger gesture. Our way, they felt, was not polite. This time, however, Elder Chang leaned forward and stabbed the air in my direction with his forefinger. "And five, now for you. Don't you be afraid, no matter what happens. God will not leave you alone. *Don't be afraid.* This is from *God!*"

I realized, then, that my guest had come with a special message for me from our merciful God. Suddenly I wanted to cling to him, to find out exactly what I should do.

"If I can't stay here, what should I do, Elder Chang?" I demanded.

"Remember God's word from Isaiah," he said. *" 'I will uphold thee!' "*

He paused briefly. "Sweep another room," he told me. "Just sweep another room."

Long after he was gone, I pondered his words. Something was going to happen to me, I realized. And probably very soon. A great peace settled over me and I was again serene, safe in the knowledge that nothing could happen to me that God did not permit.

After the model accusation meetings in Peking, it was only a week or so until the same program was initiated in our city and the frightened Lee Ahn came to tell me that he had been ordered to accuse me publicly, as my "Judas." It was only a day or two until his accusations appeared in the papers.

I had been dealt a devastating blow. My Chinese friends were so terrorized they passed by me stiffly, not daring to speak, and others wept when we met on the street. No one dared to speak openly to me or come to see me. They didn't know what terrible thing might happen to them if they were suspected of being my friend.

The Communists were determined to remove all missionaries permanently, but they had reserved a special condemnation for me.

"That American missionary is the chief American spy!" Newspapers and radios shrieked. "She is the head of the vast missionary spy activities for the imperialistic United States! She is an enemy of the People's Republic! She must be destroyed!"

I listened to them with a certain numbness. Why me? I had never been interested in politics and certainly lacked the desire and personality to accomplish any sort of espionage. But that really didn't matter. They were not after actual spies. They were destroying an ideal, an ideology they felt was harmful to their control of the people.

Considered in that light, I was the logical choice. The few missionaries from America still remaining in our city had not been in China long or had come from other parts of China and were not as likely to have as many friends among the Chinese as I. I had been in their country for twenty-five years and was well acquainted over a wide area. I had connections with two high schools and a large rural work in addition to being in the city. The later arrivals did not fit the requirements, so I was selected to be attacked both as a person and as a symbol.

"This hated American should be slowly and carefully exposed in all of China," the next day's newspaper announced.

I read the news story again, wondering just how they were going to carry out their announced purpose. I had no doubt but that they would do it. I had already learned that the Communist mind had queer convictions about truth. Merely to state a fact was to make it true. No proof was ever needed.

So the accusations continued, always under expert Communist leadership. Every school in the city was forced to hear a full account of all of the evidence of my fictional crimes. They were forced to make accusation against me and to demand the death sentence as my punishment. After every meeting of a school or neighborhood group, a special edition of

171

the newspaper was published and the blaring loudspeakers shouted my crimes from every street corner.

According to one news account, I could not be hauled into prison immediately. It was necessary to educate everyone about this horrible American imperialist first in order to stir up the greatest amount of hatred for America.

There was a set routine. A Roman Catholic priest in Shanghai was going through the same process, but he seemed to be several steps ahead of me. Each day I read of his treatment and was able to see what was in store for me. "Well, that hasn't happened to me yet," I would say to myself. "At least I'll live until that happens."

At first I found some small comfort in the fact that my publicity was only local. Soon, however, the newspapers began to quote widely separated sources of still other accounts of my evil activities. I knew then what they had meant by saying there would be information about me for all of China. Now I understood a little of what Christ experienced when He was stripped naked and held up for all to see.

Those were difficult days for me, and I was pleased when the doctor ordered me to swim every day. I was four miles from the beach, and he ordered me to walk at least one way. I knew what else he was trying to tell me. He wanted me to keep physically fit while undergoing the grueling ordeal, and he wanted to get me out of the house so I wouldn't be listening to those dreaded loudspeakers constantly drumming for my imprisonment and execution.

There was a certain amount of danger for my being out on the streets during that period; feeling was being whipped so high against me. I prepared for the trip with the care of the spy I was accused of being. I took to wearing dark glasses and pulling a big hat down over my face. I found a different way to get to the beach every day, lest an avid comrade recognize me and start a riot against me.

I entered the water and swam far out from shore. For

the first time in my life, I was not afraid of the depth. "Underneath are the everlasting arms" became my strength. There was joy and release for me in the water. And rest! I knew no Communist would swim out to get me. At last I had found a place where I could be free!

One day a Chinese friend swam over to me.

"We don't think you will be killed. We hope they will deport you." And then he paused. "And when you get out, remember us. We are still in it!"

Then he swam away, rapidly.

Repeatedly, during those days, I felt another power apart from myself and realized that Christian friends were praying for me. I had not written a letter for over a year, so God by His Spirit must have prompted the prayers. I am not a particularly brave or self-sufficient person but was kept calm and sane. Even though the pressure continued to increase, I could sleep and eat and laugh.

On one occasion, a ricksha man was pulling me home from the beach just after dusk when he spoke to me. "Are you *that* teacher?" From the constant publicity, he recognized the street location as he stopped at the gate.

"Yes," I replied.

"We are praying for you," he said softly. "Keep on praying."

He was a new Christian, not yet baptized, and was concerned about me. "Where do you go tomorrow?" he asked. "Tell me. I can take care of you."

From that evening on, no matter where or when I wanted to go out, he was there, waiting for me. He knew instinctively what to do to keep me away from crowds. He would go on unused side streets or duck into an alley in order to avoid a wild parade. I was sure that God had sent him to me. I could not have avoided trouble without him.

173

22

I knew that the end would not be long in coming. The Communists were completely predictable. The fanatical hymn of hate that was sung so loudly against me was reaching such a crescendo that they would soon be able to announce that the judgment of the people against me was so overwhelming that they had to take action.

I waited, still wrapped in His arms of peace, even though the loudspeakers were never still in their railing about me.

"Is that foreign teacher still polluting our soil? Why does the government wait? Is she to be allowed to destroy the People's Republic before they act? The People's Court has given its verdict. Kill her! Kill her! Kill her!" My so-called crimes were yelled at me from the banks of loudspeakers on the streets, wherever I walked.

The attacks against me were varied and planned to the most minute detail, calculated to isolate me from every source of comfort and help. A secret informer even went to an American friend of mine, warning him against me.

"You want to go home, don't you?" he asked. "Then don't befriend the teacher. You can't help her. You will only hurt yourself. She's dead already."

Even before the informer left, I had a call from my friend assuring me of his concern and help. That help came at great personal sacrifice and risk, but it came and I was grateful.

A rather strange thing happened one afternoon when Number One Comrade came to check some detail of mission property. It was located on a hill overlooking the bay, and there was magic about the view. I always had been touched by it.

"Look at that!" I burst out. "Isn't it beautiful?"

He looked at me for a moment in the softest mood I had ever seen in any Communist. "I believe you love China," he said.

"Of course I do. My heart is here."

I was speaking not only of my attachment to the physical beauty but of Christ's dreams for China.

Then reality closed in, and Number One Comrade was again harsh and unyielding.

Not so with a strange merchant who came into my kitchen one morning carrying a beautiful, expensive silver fox skin.

"I do not believe all of the things the papers say about you," he told me. "You are no spy. I want you to have this. Just give me some money—any amount." We both understood that the money was so he could not be accused of giving me a gift. If he were accused, he could say that he had properly skinned the foreigner by selling the fur.

It was a surprise and so lovely. I still enjoy it, but best of all I could see it was a way he had of expressing his friendship and faith in what I represented.

Not everyone believed in my innocence, however. Far from it. One of my former students came in to see me, carrying his Bible. I was sure that he had come as a friend to read a few verses of Scripture and have a brief prayer with me. Christian friends often did that at considerable risk to themselves.

But that was not his purpose.

"You are proved to be guilty." He opened his Bible. " 'If you do not repent, I will spue you out of my mouth.' " He had believed the reports and was reading to me from the book of Revelation, adding to the charge against me.

I was stunned and started to explain why I was being charged, but wisdom born of an inner prompting stopped me. Any word of mine would be used against me.

After he left I started to cry but soon stopped. *Why should I cry?* I reasoned. *Jesus had friends who deserted and killed him. Who am I to expect anything different?*

I had been trying to pack, getting ready for any eventuality, as I knew that the war against me was moving swiftly to a decision. I was occupied with that when a mission employee I will call Kaa-Li slipped into the house at night.

"I've come to tell you that the final decision is tomorrow," he said.

That did not surprise me. I had been expecting it. Indeed, it was something of a relief to know that the ordeal was to be ended soon.

"The final decision of the People's Trial is tomorrow. And I have been ordered to give crucial final evidence against you."

I was not surprised by that, either. After what had happende with Lee Ahn I had rather expected a repetition of the act.

"My wife and I have not slept for five nights," Kaa-Li went on.

I knew what deep suffering and anxiety must have filled those five days for them.

"Comrade Number One called me in and asked me many, many questions about you. And he demanded a written statement of my testimony. I sent it in, but I defended you. I said you have always been law-abiding and that you are not a spy."

I was concerned about what might happen to him for taking such a stand, but he brushed it aside.

"Now I must attend the meeting tomorrow to accuse you of using Mission money for spy work."

I couldn't keep from gasping. We both knew what was involved. A charge like that would mean the firing squad for me. If he failed to obey, it was likely that he would be killed and his wife and children would suffer unspeakable punishment. No wonder they had not slept. I could only imagine their agony.

"You are old and have no one else. I am defending you."

"But you can't!"

"I have to. My wife and I have decided that I will take prison or death or whatever they have for me."

"I can't accept that!" I told him. "You mustn't!"

But he had gone. I could do nothing!

Awe flooded my heart and mind as I stood there. What a miracle of obedience Kaa-Li was! Not because this thing he was doing related to me. Far from it! But because to do what was right, regardless of cost, was his decision.

Would I have half the courage of this young Chinese couple? Mental belief was certainly not enough to cause them to do what they were going to do. Only a deep commitment could bring that inner touch with the invisible, Almighty God to enable them to withstand and to *stand!*

I wanted to pray with someone, but it was night. It was neither safe for me to go out, nor for anyone to come to my house. So I walked out in the courtyard and alone faced the matter with God.

All the possibilities surged within my being. Death, jail, torture, the prison camp, or being torn apart by a wild-eyed mob. I opened my soul to the depths and wholly surrendered everything to God as He willed.

Instantly that same deep peace rushed back to fill my heart. Years before, shortly after I first came to China, my brother had died, and I knelt by my bed in agony.

"Why?" I asked. "Why?"

God's message for me then was direct and simple. "Trust My love."

Now, as I was alone in the courtyard, the same message came back reassuringly. "Trust My love."

I went back to my room and slept.

Kaa-Li's information was correct. The time had come for the final act in the bizarre case against me. I was not there. It wasn't necessary for the accused to be at such a trial. But I heard about it in detail later. It had been a tense and terrifying experience for my Chinese friends who were required to be present.

Trained Communist leaders and stooges shouted their hatred when the charges against me were read.

"Kill her!" they screamed. "Kill her! She is an American spy and doesn't deserve to live!"

Others took up the cry and it was some time before the courtroom quieted enough so the case could be heard. The Communists had seen a letter written by an American friend to a Chinese Christian defending me. The Chinese man, in order to save himself, accused the American letter writer of being an enemy of the State.

"That is the reason he defended her," he said, lips trembling.

Everyone thought the American would be arrested. I'm

sure he weighed that possibility himself before writing the letter. But God intervened and he was allowed to go free.

I know the Communists didn't intend it that way, but the American's letter indirectly put my case before the group. If they were going to continue the charade of affording me a fair, legal trial, the defense in that letter would have to be discredited. But they were sure they had prepared for that by calling Kaa-Li as a witness.

It was true that his written testimony had been a defense of me, but they were confident of the effect of their threats against him. He was like all the others. When he was actually faced with the choice of accusing a hated foreigner or facing prison himself they were sure he would perform according to plan.

It was with confidence that they staged another noisy demonstration against me before calling Kaa-Li to testify. "She deserves to die! Kill her! Kill her! Kill her!" That awful shouting reverberated through the court room. When it had gone on long enough in the judgment of the leaders to have its desired effect on the Christians who were forced to be there, it was halted and Kaa-Li was called to the stand.

"Do you know this hated American spy?"

"I know her," Kaa-Li replied evenly.

"Isn't it true that she used mission funds to pay for spying activities against the People's Republic of China?"

"It is not." His reply was firm and courageous. "She has not used any mission funds except for the expenses of the church. Every cent of the money spent has been accounted for."

The prosecutor was disturbed. "Isn't it true that she has been working for the imperialistic United States to help them in their plot to conquer the People's Republic?"

"No."

The questioner's eyes flashed. "You speak with some conviction, comrade." The warning in his voice was apparent. "Are you sure that you don't want to qualify that answer?"

"I do not. She is not a spy. She has not been working against China. She is a friend of our people and our nation. She does not deserve to be on trial today."

"If she's not a spy, what is she doing here in the People's Republic?"

"She is here to tell our people about God who loves them, and about Jesus Christ who died on the cross to save them."

The questioning continued angrily, but Kaa-Li was serene and unruffled. He not only defended me, but when the name of a Chinese pastor was brought up, he voluntarily defended him as well.

In the matter of a few minutes, that brave young Chinese man had destroyed the elaborate, carefully contrived plot against me. And at the same time he had restored me to Christian confidence, since the Christian leaders were all present in the courtroom.

The Communists could no longer go through with their avowed plan to execute me or even throw me in prison. I had been vindicated in the eyes of the people.

Again God intervened to keep the stalwart Kaa-Li from being taken out immediately and shot. He and his wife were to be punished severely for his spirited defense of me, but God spared their lives.

I thought this was the end of the Communist efforts to do away with me, but in that I underestimated them. The next morning, another plot was published in the paper. They knew I went to the beach every day and called for the people to mob me and kill me on the street.

I heard the cook and one of my friends talking in the kitchen but could only catch snatches of the conversation.

"Did you see the morning paper?"

"Yes," the cook whispered, "but the teacher hasn't seen it. I hid it as soon as it came."

I wondered about that but decided to remain quiet.

The cook came to talk with me later that day.

"Please, don't go out tomorrow. Just stay at home!" Horror was in his face.

"I'm only obeying the doctor," I said. "He told me to go to the beach and swim every day."

The cook was terribly upset but hurried away. Later in the day he told me of the reason for his concern. I was somewhat disturbed by it but not enough to allow it to bother my rest.

At three o'clock the next morning, I was awakened by a savage pounding on the door.

"Open the door! Open the door!"

I stirred myself sleepily. Dogs barked and lights came on in the neighborhood. They were so noisy everyone was awake. Still held strangely calm, I opened the door to the Communist police. One of them had a document in his hand.

"Come with us," he said sternly.

"Just a minute."

I had a small bag packed for such an emergency.

"You won't have to take anything along. You can come back."

But I didn't believe that.

I was taken to the police station where the superior officer sat at his desk and read the document aloud. My crimes against the State were listed in detail. It must have been the same list that formed the basis for my trial. I stood in silence, waiting for him to finish.

"Because of these crimes," he concluded, "you are sentenced to *eternal deportation,* as the worst criminal of China's history. You are never to set foot again on China soil."

I was stunned. They were deporting me! I was being sent back to America!

I still had difficulty in grasping that fact when he spoke again. "We want you to know that we have been nice to you

181

because you are old and a lady. You should have been arrested several nights ago."

As he went on talking I realized that he was talking about the night when I walked in the courtyard and surrendered all to God in prayer, and the deep peace came. Silently I thanked God for His watchcare over me.

"You can go to your home and get some things to take," he concluded.

"You mean I am to leave right away—tonight?" It wasn't possible. This had to be a cruel joke.

"We want you out of China immediately."

When we got back to my house, all of the lights were on. The communists were there already. I began preparing and choosing from the packed items I had fixed against such an eventuality as this. I was almost ready to go when I came upon a birthday card that had been sent to me by a little German girl. It had her name on it and could be evidence enough to get her in serious trouble. I looked about quickly, trying to figure how I could get it over to the stove and burn it, but that wasn't possible with an officer a few feet away. Going back through an unlighted hall I quickly tore off the name from the card and swallowed it.

Now let them look for that! I said to myself.

I started to take my radio, but they refused, saying I didn't have a pass to take it. They let me take two or three duffel bags and three smaller trunks. When the ricksha man came, however, and was loading my luggage, I tugged on his coat and pointed to the trunk with my clothes and he went and got it.

At the dock they pulled everything out of my bags and spread it out on the dock so they could know exactly what I was taking with me. Later I learned that they had to threaten the captain of the British freighter with prison unless he took me as a passenger. He wasn't prepared to take passengers, he told them. But, when that choice was given to him, he decided he could make arrangements, after all.

They had taken the keys to my car, driven it down and had parked it on the dock across the gangplank so I had to crawl over the sides of the gangplank to go aboard the ship. I realized that they wanted me to make some angry remark about the car so they would have another case against me. Fortunately, God restrained me and I got on the ship. We were underway almost immediately.

As we steamed out of the harbor I remembered that Ping had recently gotten out and had flown over a park toward some crowded apartments. He was tame. They would love him and feed him. Yes, my voice was still preaching in China! *"Knee shin Chu!* You believe the Lord!"

The Moscow radio announced the news that I had been deported; and the *New York Times* carried the item, a report of the Russian broadcast claiming that the horrible spy ring had been crushed, and that the chief spy had been deported. All in China was under control.

23

After I returned to America, I married the Reverend Perry Hanson. In Oregon the women of my denomination, who had been my loyal supporters for over twenty-five years, gave us a wedding.

Marvelous years together followed. We traveled constantly over the United States, including Alaska, urging loyalty to Christ and prayer for the persecuted Chinese Christians. Continually we found people who had been praying for us, especially during those desperate China weeks.

Those happy years brought us an even closer fellowship with Christ. Then in 1967 Mr. Hanson went home to be with Christ and the Christian assurance and joy contrasted sharply with the old piercing death-wail of China.

I was most concerned about Kaa-Li and his wife who had so courageously saved my life in China at great personal sacrifice. Years went by before I learned the extent of their suffering. Even now I have to guess at much of it.

After I was deported, Kaa-Li and his wife went through indescribable mental torture. The brave young couple lived under constant terror for a year and a half. He was not allowed to have a job. No one spelled that out to him. It was accomplished by more subtle means. Employers did not dare to hire him because he had spoken out to protect the spy who was accused by the highest authorities. He was charged with having accepted money from me to carry out illegal activities.

His wife, who taught school, was under daily accusation and shame from the school authorities. Every effort was used in an attempt to force her to turn Communist. This technique of breaking the will to resist was developed to the highest extent and was controlled by the Chief Public Security Officer who held the power of life and death. He and his men were the most feared in all of China.

The Communists were in no hurry. If Kaa-Li and his wife did not break in a week the pressure would be exerted for a month or three times that. They were forced to undergo horrible accusation and self-confession meetings separately. Every night for a month, both of them were quizzed individually about every detail of their lives from the age of eight years up to the day the Communists took control of their city. Then their answers were compared by the comrades.

Following that month, every night for two more months they were forced through detailed grillings and "confessions" about what they had done since the Communists took power. They were forced to publicly humiliate and ridicule themselves for real and imaginary shortcomings, which were always followed by a storm of hisses, unreasonable questions, and absurd criticism from the assembly led by the officials.

They had to pay careful attention to all of this, as their oral and written confessions for the next day's meetings had to include answers and comments on those former questions and criticisms. After those separate meetings they were allowed to go home, where they worked, sometimes until as late as three or four in the morning, to prepare written statements for the continuation the next evening.

After such self-castigation and the unremitting goadings from the crowd at the meetings, they confessed to being obsessed with "serious petty bourgeois thoughts," "individualism," "not loving the Communist State as God," "Americanamania," and to being "American running dogs."

They flatly denied spying or any other illegal activity. At the end of this period, Kaa-Li was physically crushed and his wife fainted at a meeting. They accused her of pretense, but finally she was surprisingly and unexpectedly hospitalized and the charges against her were temporarily dropped. For three months she hovered at the brink of death. The Communist cadre leader who came to check on her said, "There's no need to kill her. She's going to die, anyway."

Finally, as she was beginning to respond to treatment, the government dropped the charges against them for lack of evidence.

As soon as she was well, they got away to a distant city where they were strangers. They were free, but money was an acute problem. After seven different moves involving several months, eventually they were able to find a way to begin life again. The time came when they, too, were able to escape to a freer land.

I had asked Kaa-Li once if he were ever bitter over the suffering because I had stayed.

"I've never thought of that," he said, "even once. If we hadn't suffered, we would never have known God as we know Him now. We would never have learned to depend on Him alone."

Awe fills my heart at the price this couple had to pay for refusing to be my accusers and so saving my life. The glory shines the brightest in the greatest darkness. Every breath I draw today, I owe to them. How does one repay for life itself?

The "Judas" suffered horrible agony of soul. Word later reached me that his hair turned absolutely white. He too needs loving prayer.

I think back to my youth, the time when God first began to speak to me of being a missionary and how reluctant I had been. I can say with Kaa-Li that it was the committing of my will to God that brought fulfillment and joy. To work in partnership with God—to let Him break through in prayer and service—is the greatest adventure life can offer.

Today God is still breaking through in China. The years of calling for prayer for the Christians and the 800 million Chinese have resulted in an incredible, growing underground church in China. May God rule and overrule, that all recent happenings work out to His glory and bring freedom for Christian worship again in the great land I love.

Joyously

Let God use Us to set off
  His firecracker of change.
To light the candle of Love,
To love as Christ Loved--
  to the Death.

Tell of Christ's Cross to millions
  who have never heard.

The Climax Picture of
"The Wheelborrow and the Comrade"

Mrs. Perry (Irene) Hanson
Westminster Gardens
1420 Santa Domingo Drive
Duarte, California 91010